How to Develop A Rugby Union Coach

(Book No.16)

Develop A Player

Disclaimer
The information in this book is meant to supplement, not replace, proper rugby union training. Like any sport involving speed, equipment, balance and environmental factors, playing the sport of rugby poses some inherent risks. The authors and publisher advise readers to take full responsibility for their safety and know their limits. Before practicing the skills described in this book, be sure your equipment is well-maintained and do not take risks beyond your level of experience, aptitude, training or comfort level.

Copyright
Copyright © 2019, David Christopher Miles All rights reserved. All rights reserved. Apart from any permitted use under AUS copyright law, no part of this publication may be reproduced or transmitted in any form or by any means, electronic or mechanical, including photocopying, recording, or any information, storage or retrieval system, without permission in writing from the publisher or under license from the Author. Copyright Licensing Agency Limited. Printed in AUS for Develop A Player by Develop A Player.

ISBN-13: 978-0-6482745-5-1

Acknowledgement
Firstly, and foremost my three wonderful children, Alex, Bethan and Max who are everything in my life.

To the Dubai Book Club for good moral debate and giggles.

And to Rugby, for the joy of mates, beer and happiness.

Develop A Player

Purpose
The purpose of this book is to provide developing coaches with the information needed to become excellent in the sport of Rugby Union

Objectives
The objectives of this book are:

- ☑ To provide the reader with an understanding of the forward and backs and their function in the game

- ☑ To understand the core skills of the game

- ☑ To develop the essential skills for great coach development

- ☑ To provide an insight into shapes, structures, defensive structures and tactics of the game

- ☑ To provide FREE access to a professional coach development portal **www.developaplayer.com** whereby the coach can record and share their coach development with players, scouts and managers.

Table Of Contents

Chapter 1: 9
The Origins of Rugby 9
- History of Rugby Football 9
- The Calcutta Cup 11
- The Bledisloe Cup 13
- The Six Nations (Northern Hemisphere) 14
- The Championship (Southern Hemisphere) 15
- The World Cup 16

Chapter 2: 18
The Game of Rugby Union 18
- How the game is played 18
- The rules of the game 18
  - Principals of play 19
  - Scoring points 19
  - Restarts in the game 19
  - The playing field 20
- Modified rules for different age groups 21
  - Under 6s'/ 7s' 21
  - Under 8s' / 9s' 22
  - Under 10s' / 11s' 22
  - Under 12s' 23
  - Under 13s' to Under 19s' 23

Chapter 3: 25
What is a Coach 25
- The purpose and role of a Coach 25
- Understanding player development 25
  - How the rugby brain works 26

The role of natural testosterone in sports development 27
So why become a Coach? **28**

Chapter 4: 29

Coaching Principals for Excellence 29

Coaches Self Reflection **29**
    Pre-Game 36
    During-Game 37
    Post-Game 38
Coaching Principles **39**
Coaching Excellence **41**

Chapter 5: 42

The Forwards 42

The Forwards, their role, and function **43**
The Front Row **44**
    Loose-Head Prop (No.1) – LHP 44
    Hooker (No.2) - H 45
    Tight-head Prop (No.3) - THP 46
The Second Row **47**
    Loose-lock (No. 4) - LL 47
The Back Row **49**
    Blindside Flanker (No. 6) - BF 49
    Openside Flanker (No. 7) – OF 50
    Number 8 (No. 8) – 8 51
The Scrum **55**
    Scenarios where a scrum takes place 56
    Offside lines created from a scrum 59
    The formation of a scrum 61
The Lineout **63**
    Scenarios where a lineout takes place 64
    Offside lines created from a lineout 65
    Lineout options 66
    Lineout Calls 69

Chapter 6: 72
The Backs 72

   The Backs, their role, and function 73
   The Half Backs 74
      Scrum-half (No. 9) - SH..74
      Outside-half (No.10) – OH 76
   The Inside Backs 78
      Inside Centre (No.12) – IC 78
      Outside Centre (No.13) – OC 80
   The Outside Backs 81
      Blindside Winger (No.11) – BF..81
      Openside Winger (No.14) – OW 83
      Fullback (No.15) - F..84
   Attacking moves by the backs 87
      Attacking principal 1- Create attack space 88
      Attacking principal 2 – Create overloads..................................89
      Attacking principal 3 – Create mismatches 90
   Defensive structures by the backs 91
      Defence principal 1 – Man on Man Marking...........................92
      Defence principal 2 – Umbrella 93
      Defence principal 3 – Drift 94
      Defence principal 4 – Smother 95

Chapter 7: 96
Open play Rugby 96

   Field Segmentation...96
   Structures..99
   Shapes...102
      Strategies and Tactics 103
   How to maintain continuity of play 105
   Pros' and Cons' of structure v heads up Rugby.......................107

Chapter 8: 109

Core skills 109
Catch and Pass skills development 109
The mechanics of passing the rugby ball 110
Tackling Skills Development 111
Front on tackle (passive) 111
Front on tackle (active) 112
Side on tackle 112
Rear tackle 113
Smother tackle 114
Continuity Skills Development 115
Kicking Skills Development 116
The distance kick 116
The cross-field kick 117
The grubber kick 117
The chip kick 118
The conversion 119
Other kicks 119

Chapter 9: 121

Essential skills for developing players .121
Attacking rugby 122
Attacking with the ball in possession 123
Attacking without the ball in possession 123
Defensive rugby 124
Defending set pieces 125
Defending broken play 126
Physical Conditioning 127
General physical conditioning 128
Mental Strength 128
The influencers on the four disciplines 132
5 Rules for supportive parents and care givers 133
Coaches 134

Chapter 10: 137

My greatest players **137**
   My journey as a Coach..**137**
   The Forwards...**138**
      My greatest Loose-head Prop - LHP.......................................**138**
      My greatest Hooker - H..**139**
      My greatest Tight-head Prop - THP..**140**
      My Greatest Loose Lock - LL..**142**
      My Greatest Tight Lock - TL...**143**
      My Greatest Blindside Flanker – BF..**145**
      My Greatest Openside Flanker – OF.......................................**146**
      My Greatest Number 8 – 8..**147**
   The Backs..**148**
      My Greatest Scrum-half – SH...**148**
      My Greatest Outside-half – OH...**149**
      My Greatest Inside Centre – IC..**151**
      My Greatest Outside Centre – OC...**152**
      My Greatest Blindside Winger – BW.......................................**153**
      My Greatest Openside Winger – OW.....................................**154**
      My Greatest Fullback – F..**155**

Other Books in the Series **157**
   The Front Row...**157**
   The Second Row **157**
   The Back Row **157**
   The Half-backs...**158**
   The Inside Backs **158**
   The Outside Backs **158**

The Development Portal **160**

Chapter 1:
The Origins of Rugby

Chapter Objectives:
In this chapter you will gain knowledge of the following:

- ☑ **History of Rugby Football**
- ☑ **The Calcutta Cup**
- ☑ **The Bledisloe Cup**
- ☑ **The Six Nations (Northern Hemisphere)**
- ☑ **The Championship (Southern Hemisphere)**
- ☑ **The World Cup**

History of Rugby Football

The origins of the game, now known across the world simply as rugby, can be traced back over 2000 years. The Romans played a ball game called *harpastum,* a word derived from the Greek word "seize", the implication of the name being that somebody actually carried or handled the ball.

More recently, in medieval England, documents record young men leaving work early to compete for their village or town in games of football. Laws were passed, in Tudor times, forbidding the *"devilish pastime"* of football, as too many injuries and fatalities seriously depleted the available workforce. The participants of this *devilish pastime* are recorded thus... "The players are young men from 18-30 or upwards; married as well as single and many veterans who retain a relish for the sport are occasionally seen in the very heat of the conflict..." A description that some might say is as applicable today as it was all of those years ago.

Shrove Tuesday became the traditional timing for such conflicts. Rules differed from one part of the country to the next, from Derbyshire to Dorset to Scotland, records reveal many regional variations to the game. The games often took place over an ill-defined pitch – the ball being kicked, carried and driven through town and village streets over fields, hedges and streams.

The roots to the modern game of rugby can be traced to a school for *young gentlemen* in the Midlands of England, which in 1749 finally outgrew its cramped surroundings within the town centre and moved to a new site on the edge of the town of Rugby in Warwickshire. The new Rugby School site had "…every accommodation that could be required for the exercise of young gentlemen." This eight-acre plot became known as the Close.

The game of football, which was played on the Close between 1749 and 1823, had very few rules: touchlines were introduced, and the ball could be caught and handled, but running with ball in hand was not permitted. Progress forward towards the opposition's goal was generally made by kicking. Games could last for five days and often included more than 200 boys. For fun, 40 seniors may take on two hundred younger pupils, the seniors having prepared for the event by first sending their boots to the town cobbler to have extra thick soles put on them, bevelled at the front to better slice into the shins of the enemy!

It was during a match on the Close in the autumn of 1823 that the face of the game changed to the one which is recognisable today. A local historian described this historic event as follows: "with a fine disregard for the rules of the game as played in his time, William Webb Ellis first took the ball in his arms and ran with it, thus originating the distinctive feature of the Rugby game." Ellis had apparently caught the ball and, according to the rules of the day, should have moved backwards giving himself enough room to either punt the ball up field or to place it for a kick at goal. He would have been protected from the opposing team as they could only advance to the spot where the ball had been caught. In disregarding this rule Ellis had caught the ball and instead of retiring, had run forward, ball in hand towards the opposite goal. A dangerous move and one that would not find its way into the fast-developing rule book until 1841.

The rules and the fame of the game spread quickly as the Rugby School boys moved onwards and upwards, first to the universities of Oxford and Cambridge. The first university match was played in 1872. From the universities, the graduating teachers introduced the game to other English, Welsh and Scottish schools, and overseas postings for the Old Rugbeians who had moved through to the army officer class, promoted its growth on the international stage. Scotland played England in the first International game at Raeburn Place, Edinburgh in 1871.

The Calcutta Cup

The Six Nations Championships date back to 1883 in its original guise as the Home Nations Championships, when it was contested by England, Ireland, Scotland and Wales. More recently, trophies have been awarded for a number of individual competitions during the Six Nations including the Millennium Trophy which is awarded to the winner of the game between England and Ireland; the Giuseppe Garibaldi Trophy which is awarded to the winner of the game between France and Italy and the Centenary Quaich which is awarded to the winner of the game between Scotland and Ireland.

However, the Calcutta Cup pre-dates all of the other Six Nations trophies and indeed the competition itself

Develop A Player

Following the popular introduction of rugby to India in 1872, the Calcutta (Rugby) Football Club was established by former students of Rugby School in January 1873, joining the Rugby Football Union in 1874. However, with the departure of a local British army regiment (and perhaps more crucially the cancellation of the free bar at the club!), interest in rugby diminished.

Whilst the Calcutta (Rugby) Football Club was disbanded in 1878, members decided to keep the memory of the club alive by having the remaining 270 silver rupees in their bank account melted down to be made into a trophy. The trophy was then presented to the Rugby Football Union (RFU) to be used as "the best means of doing some lasting good for the cause of Rugby Football."

The trophy, which stands at approximately 18 inches (45 cm) high, sits on a wooden base whose plates hold the date of each match played; the winning country and the names of both team captains. The silver cup is delicately etched and decorated with three king cobras who form the handles of the cup and sitting atop the circular lid is an Indian elephant.

The original trophy is still in existence but years of mistreatment (including a drunken kick about in 1988 on Princes Street in Edinburgh by the England player Dean Richards and the Scottish player John Jeffry in which the trophy was used as the ball) have left it too fragile to be moved from its permanent home at the Museum of Rugby in Twickenham. Instead both England and Scotland have full size models of the cup to be displayed by the winning team and when England are the victors the original trophy is displayed by the Museum of Rugby in a purpose-built trophy cabinet with revolving stand.

The Calcutta Club had thought that the trophy would be used as an annual prize for club competitions, similarly to the Football

Develop A Player

FA Cup which was introduced around the same time. Indeed in 1884 the Calcutta Cricket and Football Club re-established rugby in Calcutta in 1884 and a club trophy called the Calcutta Rugby Union Challenge Cup – which also became known as the Calcutta Cup – was introduced in 1890. However, the RFU preferred to keep the competition at international level to retain the 'gentlemanly' rather than competitive nature of the sport and run the risk of a move to professionalism.

As Wales didn't have a national team and Ireland's team lagged far behind the English and Scottish sides, the Calcutta Cup became the victor's trophy in the annual England versus Scotland game following its arrival in the UK in 1878. Since the first game in 1879 (which was declared a draw) England has won 54% of the 118 matches played and Scotland 39%, with 13% of matches ending in a draw between the two sides. Annual matches between the two sides have continued every year since, with the exception of the World War years between 1915-1919 and 1940-1946. The venue for the match is always the Murrayfield Stadium in Scotland during even years and the Twickenham Stadium in England during odd years.

With the introduction of the Home Nations competition in 1883 and the vast improvement in the Irish and Welsh sides it was suggested that the Calcutta Cup went to the winner of the Home Nations competition. However, the tradition of the trophy going to the victors of the England versus Scotland game was a popular one and the suggestion was overruled.

The Bledisloe Cup

Rugby Union's Bledisloe Cup is contested between Australia's Wallabies and New Zealand's All Blacks. It is named after Lord Bledisloe, the Governor-General of New Zealand who donated the trophy in 1931.

There is some conjecture as to when the first Bledisloe Cup match was played. The Australian Rugby Union contends that the one-off 1931 match played at Eden Park was first. However, no firm evidence has been produced to support this claim, and the New Zealand Rugby Football Union believes that the first match was when New Zealand toured Australia in 1932. Between 1931 and 1981 it was contested irregularly in the course of rugby tours between the two countries. New Zealand won it 19 times and Australia 4 times in this period.

In the years 1982 to 1995, it was contested annually, sometimes as a series of three matches and other times in a single match. During these years New Zealand won it 11 times and Australia 3 times.

Since 1996, the cup has been contested as part of the annual Tri Nations tournament. The Tri Nations brings South Africa in as the third team. Until 1998 the cup was contested in a three-match series: the two Tri Nations matches between these sides and an additional third match. New Zealand won these series in 1996 and 1997, and Australia won it in 1998. During this three-year period, with the 1998 the exception, dead rubbers weren't contested.

In 2012 the rugby championship came into effect with Argentina entering the competition

The Six Nations (Northern Hemisphere)

The Six Nations Championship is one of the biggest dates in the rugby union calendar bringing together the best sides in Europe.

Develop A Player

England, Wales, Ireland, France, Scotland and Italy compete every year for the prestigious championship trophy. Originally formed as the Home Nations Championship in 1883, the competition has blossomed over the years and became its current format in 2000 when Italy joined the Five Nations.

The idea of the Six Nations first began way back in 1883 when England, Scotland, Ireland and Wales competed in the Home Nations Championship. The first two years were dominated by England and Scotland before Wales came to the fore winning four titles between 1905 and 1909. When then the Home Nations ended in 1939 both Wales and Scotland racked up 11 championships each.

Rugby, along with many other sports, took a back seat between 1940 and 1946 as World War II raged across Europe. When it returned in 1947, the Home Nations had evolved into the Five Nations as France were added into the mix. It took the French a few years to get into their stride, sharing their first title in 1954 with England and Wales

However, once they claimed their first outright crown in 1959, they came into their own. The 1960s and 1970s saw France dominate with Les Bleus winning no less than eight titles during this period. The Five Nations continued right up to the new millennium before it was rebranded once again.

The Championship (Southern Hemisphere)

The Rugby Championship is an international rugby union competition contested annually by Argentina, Australia, New Zealand, and South Africa.

Develop A Player

Australia and New Zealand first played each other in 1903. South Africa toured both nations in 1921 but there was never any formal competition between these teams.

The inaugural Tri Nations tournament was in 1996 and was won by New Zealand – known as the All Blacks. South Africa won their first title in 1998, and Australia their first in 2000. Following the last Tri Nations tournament in 2011, New Zealand had won ten championships, with South Africa and Australia on three titles each. The first Rugby Championship was won by New Zealand, who won all six of their matches.

The series is played on a home-and-away basis. From the first tournament in 1996 until 2005, the three teams played each other twice. Since then, each team has played the others three times, except in the Rugby World Cup years when the series is decided by a double round-robin

The World Cup

The Rugby World Cup is contested every four years between the top international teams. The tournament was first held in 1987, when the tournament was co-hosted by New Zealand and Australia.

The winners are awarded the Webb Ellis Cup, named after William Webb Ellis, the Rugby School pupil who, according to a popular legend, invented rugby by picking up the ball during a football game.

Prior to the Rugby World Cup, there was no truly global rugby union competition, but there were a number of other tournaments.

Develop A Player

Rugby Union was also played at the Summer Olympic Games, first appearing at the 1900 Paris games and subsequently at London in 1908, Antwerp in 1920, and Paris again in 1924. France won the first gold medal, then Australasia, with the last two being won by the United States. However, the sport ceased to be on the Olympic program after 1924 thus making the USA the current and reigning Olympic champions in the game of Rugby Union!

Chapter 2:
The Game of Rugby Union

Overview
In this chapter you will gain knowledge of the following:

- ☑ **How is the game played?**
- ☑ **The rules of the game**
- ☑ **Modified rules for different age groups**

How the game is played

When someone new to the game asks, what is rugby, and how is it played? The various responses are;

"It's like soccer, but you can pick the ball up and pass it".
……..Or…..It's like American Football but without all the helmets and protective gear………Or …. Ermm…… urhhhhhh……. I don't really know….. maybe there's a book somewhere that can explain how the game is played but also how to coach the game as well.

Well you're in luck ☺ because this book does that, and a whole lot more.

The rules of the game
There are many rules that govern the game of Rugby Union for which a completely separate book could be written detailing which ones are great, which ones are 'ok' and which ones seem to have been concocted after several glasses of good wine!

Develop A Player

In essence though there are a few core principals of play, three ways to score points, and four ways to restart the game.

Principals of play
- Rugby is a game of evasion, not contact.
- Each team can start with 15 players and up to 7 substitutes.
- The ball must be passed backwards and carried forward.

Scoring points
- **A try** - five points are awarded for touching the ball down in your opponent's goal area.
- **A conversion** - two points are added for a successful kick through the goalposts after a try.
- **A goal kick** - three points are awarded for a penalty kick or drop goal through the posts.
- **Passing** – In general play, the ball must be passed backwards, not forwards.

Restarts in the game
- **Scrum** – A scrum is used to restart the game when there has been a technical error in play.
- **Lineout** – A lineout is used to restart the game when the ball has gone out of the field of play.
- **Score restart** – When one team has scored, the ball is carried back to the half-way line and kicked off again.
- **Game Restart** – At the start of the game, and at the start of the second half, the ball is carried back to the half-way line and kicked off.

The playing field

A typical length of a rugby field is 100m for the field of play plus the depth of the in-goal areas at both ends of the field, say 10m each - total 120m. The width is typically 70m so the area = 120m x 70m = 8400 sq. m. A full-size pitch (22m in-goal) would be 144m x 70m = 10080 sq. m

The major lines across the field's length are the 50-meter line, also referred to as the half-way line, the 22-meter line, the try line and the dead-ball line. The minor lines across the field are the 10-meter line.

The major lines running the length of the field are the side-lines. The minor lines are the 5-meter line. There is also a marker at the 15-meter line in from touch. The purpose of the 5-meter line and the 15-meter lines are to govern the area in which the forwards must stand when restarting the game from a lineout.

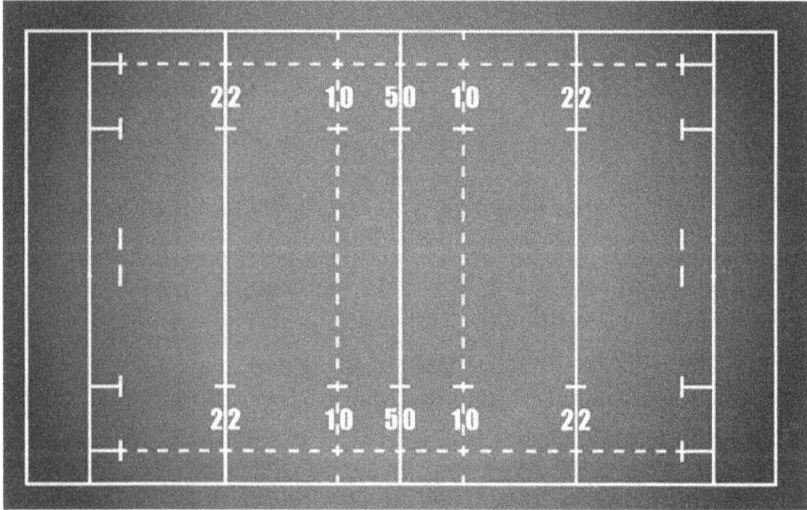

Develop A Player

Modified rules for different age groups

Being able to run is essential. Rugby, after all, is an active game, and to be able to enjoy the game, the young athlete must have a sufficient base level of physical conditioning to be able to compete for the duration of each match.

However, it is unfair to expect a six-year-old player just new to the game to be thrown into a full-sized pitch covering the same distances during a match as a full professional international player.

Modified field sizes, playing time, playing numbers and rules have therefore been developed to aid in the development of young players aligned to the concept of Long-Term Player Development (LTPD).

Under 6s'/ 7s'
- Field size = 50m x 25m
- Playing time = 15-minute halves
- Playing numbers = 7 per side
- Modified Rules:
    - Ball Size 2
    - Scoring A try is worth 5 points.
    - No conversion attempt after a try
    - No penalty goals or drop goals at this level
    - Kick-off - Taken in the form of a "place-kick".
    - Non-scoring team to kick off.
    - No kicking is allowed in general play.
    - A "Tackle" is deemed when a defending player makes contact with the ball carrier with two hands (simultaneously) below waist height.
    - Scrums and Line outs – U7 may choose to play these depending on coaches' agreements.

Develop A Player

Under 8s' / 9s'
- Field size = 70m x 35m (half field)
- Playing time = 15-minute halves (20 minutes for U9s')
- Playing numbers = 7 per side (10 per side for U9s')
- Modified Rules:
    - Ball Size 3
    - Scoring A try is worth 5 points.
    - Kick-off - Taken in the form of a "place -kick".
    - Non-scoring team to kick off 5-meters.
    - No kicking is allowed in general play.
    - A tackle occurs when the ball carrier is brought to the ground and held by an opponent.
    - Scrums are non-contested with five-player scrum, U9 has no No. 8
    - Lineouts are non-contested.

Under 10s' / 11s'
- Field size = 120m x 60m (Cones placed 5 meters in from touch on a standard field)
- Playing time = 20-minute halves
- Playing numbers = 12 per side
- Modified Rules:
    - Ball Size 4
    - Scoring a try is worth 5 points. A kick at goal following a try is worth 2 points.
    - There are no penalty goals or drop goals in Midi Rugby
    - Kick-off - taken in the form of a "place -kick". The ball must travel 10 m towards their opponent's goal line.
    - Restart "Drop kick" by non-scoring team after a try. Non –scoring team to restart.
    - Kicking is allowed in general play.

Develop A Player

- o A tackle occurs when the ball carrier is brought to the ground and held by an opponent.
- o Six player scrum is contested. Maximum one-meter push.
- o The lineout is contested, however no lifting or supporting.

Under 12s'
- Field size = 120m x 70m.
- Playing time = 25-minute halves.
- Playing numbers = 15 per side.
- Modified Rules:
    - o Ball Size 4
    - o Scoring a try is worth 5 points. A kick at goal following a try is worth 2 points.
    - o There are no penalty goals or drop goals in Midi Rugby.
    - o Kick-off - taken in the form of a "place -kick". The ball must travel 10 m towards their opponent's goal line.
    - o Restart "Drop kick" by non-scoring team after a try. Non –scoring team to restart.
    - o Kicking is allowed in general play.
    - o A tackle occurs when the ball carrier is brought to the ground and held by an opponent.
    - o Eight player scrum is contested. Maximum one metre push.
    - o The lineout is contested, however no lifting or supporting.

Under 13s' to Under 19s'
- Field size = 120m x 70m
- Playing time = 35-minute halves
- Playing numbers = 15 per side

Develop A Player

- Modified Rules:
  - Play a full field with 15 players using a full-size ball.
  - Each team has no more than 15 players in the playing area during play.
  - A match organiser may authorise matches to be played with fewer than 15 players in each team
  - For international matches, a union may nominate up to eight replacements. For other matches, the match organiser decides how many replacements may be nominated, up to a maximum of eight.
  - Scrums will become uncontested if either team cannot field a suitably trained front row or if the referee so orders.
  - Tactically replaced players may return to play only when replacing:
    - An injured front-row player.
    - A player with a blood injury.
    - A player with a head injury.
    - A player who has just been injured as a result of foul play (as verified by the match officials).
  - A match organiser may implement rolling tactical replacements at defined levels of the game within its jurisdiction. The number of interchanges must not exceed 12.

Chapter 3:
What is a Coach

Overview
In this chapter you will gain knowledge of the following:

- ☑ **The purpose and role of a Coach**
- ☑ **Understanding player development**
- ☑ **So why become a Coach**

The purpose and role of a Coach

The purpose of coaching is to improve the individual's performance in their chosen sport. This involves either enhancing current skills or acquiring new skills. Once the player successfully acquires the skills, the coach is no longer needed. Mentoring is development driven.

The role of the coach is to assist the player in developing them to their full potential. They are responsible for training players in a sport by analyzing their performances, instructing in relevant skills and by providing encouragement. But you are also responsible for the guidance of the athlete in life and their chosen sport.

Understanding player development

The brain is an amazing thing. An athlete who wants to be the best they can be in a sport they love is equally as amazing. Both need to be understood, nurtured and allowed to develop over time.

Develop A Player

By understanding the brain, the player, coach, and supportive family members can help both the brain and the player achieve truly awesome things.

The brain grows like a tub of sprouts left in the sun. Brain cells get longer and make new connections. The left half of the cortex grows slower than the right in all human babies, but in males, it develops over a longer period, with the female hormone oestrogen promoting faster growth in girls than boys. As the right half of the cortex grows, it tries to make connections with the left half. In boys, the left half of the brain isn't ready to make the connection.

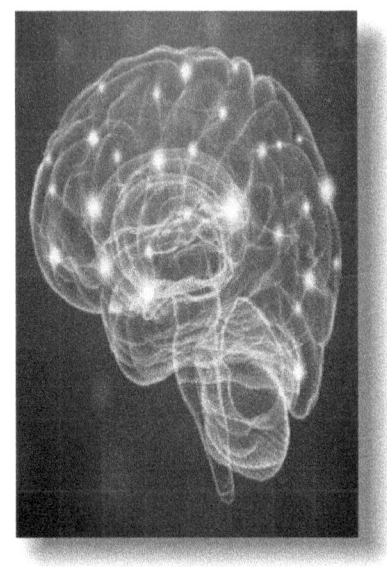

After reaching out to the left and being unable to plug in, the right half stays where it is. As a result, the right half of a boy's brain is richer in internal connections but poorer in cross connections to the other half of the brain. It is therefore clear that regular practice actually helps the brain's connections to connect permanently, so encouragement and teaching affect the shape and power of the brain in later life. So why is this important to know?

How the rugby brain works
Our brains are brilliant and flexible devices that are always learning. Parents normally teach a young boy how to avoid getting into fights and how to solve disputes peacefully, reinforcing that knocking someone over is not tolerated.

Develop A Player

Coaches, who aren't aware of the brain's development, ask these same young developing players to forget all those early social rules, so delicately taught, and demand that they go out onto the field of play and be a dynamic and unstoppable rugby sensation. Some boys are ready for this challenge and take to it like a duck to water, however to other this can be challenging and therefore need a little more time, and a little more nurturing from their parents and coaches before they are ready to compete to the fullest of their ability.

At these early stages of a young man's rugby career we can normally identify four types of rugby players:
- The "**Thinker**" who eats, breathes and sleeps rugby.
- The "**Bulldozer**" who loves the physical game.
- The "**Star**" who is expected to be playing rugby.
- The "**Developing**" kid who is not yet sure why he is playing rugby.

The role of natural testosterone in sports development
Testosterone in varying degrees affects every boy. It gives a boy growth spurts, makes him want to be active, and makes him competitive. Testosterone triggers significant changes:
- Around the age of 4 – Initial activity and boyishness
- Around the age of 12 – In rapid growth and disorientation
- Around the age of 14 – Is testing limits and breaking through to early manhood

The boy with testosterone in his bloodstream likes to know who the boss is, but also wants to be treated fairly. Bad environments bring out the worst in him. The boy with lots of testosterone needs strong guidance and a safe, ordered environment to help him develop his rugby ability and leadership is needed to channel his rugby enthusiasm productively.

Develop A Player

Boys need to learn empathy and feeling and be shown tenderness if they are to progress in life's journey. As the rugby player develops, he does not need ridicule and blame from his parents or coach. It is important that these role models provide understanding and support. It is our job to honour and steer a young man in a healthy direction if he is to become a well-rounded rugby player for the future.

There is hope for all the four types of rugby players as natural windows of accelerated developmental exist which the player, parent and coach should be mindful of and be ready to take full advantage of in the pursuit of sporting excellence. Chapter 8 takes a look at these developmental windows in greater detail.

So why become a Coach?

The Coach has a role in building the whole person by ensuring that playing Rugby is an enjoyable experience in the player's life journey. The position of rugby coach is incredibly important to the health of the game, with many professional players ever thankful for that one person who mentored them at the very start. You might be a parent whose child loves rugby, or a former player looking to turn their love of the oval ball into a career, or even a current player who wants to give something back and/or net some extra income.

It may also be that you wish to cross codes, playing union but learning to coach league, or vice versa – learning how to teach others the intricacies of rugby will always improve your own game awareness and strategy. Whatever your circumstances, rugby coaching is a rewarding endeavour for those committed to passing on passion to other rugby devotees.

Chapter 4:
Coaching Principals for Excellence

Chapter Objectives:
In this chapter you will gain knowledge of the following:

- ☑ **Coaches Self Reflection**
- ☑ **Coaching Principles**
- ☑ **Coaching Excellence**

Overview
The ability to objectively, and to be intelligently critical of your own coaching performance is the first step to becoming an excellent coach.

This is by no means that the developing coach needs to beat himself up every time he does not win a game, it is more so that through a systematic analysis process the coach can continuously improve his coaching abilities.

Coaches Self Reflection

The below simple step process takes the coach through the various elements of the self-reflection:

- **Step 1 – On Field** (analysis of on-field coaching)
  With every game comes a great opportunity to learn and develop how to be a better coach during the game.

Develop A Player

By using the below matrix, a coach can gain valuable insight into what he/she needs to do to continuously improve and deliver better results to the team.

Positives – Things I do well are:	Areas I can improve and develop skills in:
e.g. Technical know-how of the scrum	e.g. coaching my side on how to kick under pressure
Constraints / Limitations that prevent me from being as effective as I can be are:	**Opportunities available for me to improve my on-field coaching are:**
e.g. head coach not seeking my input during a game	e.g. mid-field attacking moves

- **Step 2 – Coaching Effectiveness**
  In addition to your on-field coaching, your behaviour, and skills in several key areas have an impact on your effectiveness as a rugby coach.

Develop A Player

As a coach it is vital to develop a rapport with the players. This does not mean you have to be their best friend, but it does mean that a mutual respect needs to be established. The following table will help the developing coach get an objective look at his/her current relationship approach with the players.

Key: 1 = Ineffective; 2 = Moderately ineffective; 3 = Adequate; 4 = Moderately effective; 5 = Effective

	Working directly with players					
1	I provide positive and constructive feedback to each player during training	1	2	3	4	5
2	I involve the players in decision making during training	1	2	3	4	5
3	I ensure players UNDERSTAND the technical /tactical/strategic corrections and decisions I make during training sessions	1	2	3	4	5
4	I am available to each player after training and games to discuss their issues	1	2	3	4	5
5	I understand when and how to talk to each player before games	1	2	3	4	5

A coach must also ensure that his coaching program is understood and supported by not only the players, but the entire management and support staff. The below table will help the

Develop A Player

coach understand the wider considerations needed for the coaching program.

	Support of my coaching program					
1	I am able to store and retrieve information on the players	1	2	3	4	5
2	I maintain regular contact and communications with the sport science / sport medicine staff	1	2	3	4	5
3	I ensure players are properly seeking out 'life balance' and non-rugby activities	1	2	3	4	5
4	I have a comprehensive, detailed written plan for each season	1	2	3	4	5
5	I get to know each player as an individual and a person	1	2	3	4	5

Develop A Player

Going beyond the support of the coaching program the coach needs to understand that to maintain the support throughout the season, this is where an appreciation of good program management and stakeholder management and communications needs to be understood.

	Program Management					
1	I ensure that everyone involved in my coaching process i.e. staff, players, other coaches, team managers etc. clearly understand what is expected of them	1	2	3	4	5
2	I have a strong and positive relationship with the management of the organisation	1	2	3	4	5
3	I make time each year for professional development	1	2	3	4	5
4	I ensure that players are taking responsibility for themselves and their preparation i.e. being professional	1	2	3	4	5
5	I can alter / adapt the program if weather, injury, change in training time / venue impacts on the player training	1	2	3	4	5

Develop A Player

Once the rapport with the players is understood, the support for the program has been assessed and the stakeholder engagement is considered, the coach then needs to assess the current level of commitment to continuously improve those key elements of coaching excellence.

Strategic Skills							
1	I ensure each player is able to identify their own and the overall team goal	1	2	3	4	5
2	When the team is not performing, I handle the pressure well	1	2	3	4	5
3	I have a clear understanding of world trends in Rugby and what our leading competitors are doing	1	2	3	4	5
4	I formally evaluate the progress of each player and the team each season	1	2	3	4	5
5	I look to be innovative in my integration of support services to gain a performance edge over competitors	1	2	3	4	5

Develop A Player

- **Step 3 – Game day coaching**
  Some coaches are absolutely brilliant at the first two steps, with great on field coaching, and coaching effectiveness, however on game day the same coolness and focus gets lost. Critical analysis therefore needs to be done to evaluate the coaching performance during each of the three key game day coaching periods.

Before a game commences the following table can be used to develop the coach, taking into consideration the three concepts of; *what do you do well*, *what needs improving*, *what can you start doing.*

Develop A Player

Pre-Game			
Activity	What do I do well	What do I believe needs improving	Strategies to achieve improvement
Pre-Game player briefing			
Individual player instructions			
Interaction with team coaches, head coach			
Interaction with support staff, team management			

Develop A Player

During-Game			
Activity	What do I do well	What do I believe needs improving	Strategies to achieve improvement
Behaviour during game			
Analysis of game and players			
Decision making under pressure			
Feedback to players during ½ time			
Interaction with coaches and support staff			

Post-Game			
Activity	What do I do	What do I	Strategies to

Develop A Player

	well	believe needs improving	achieve improvement
Feedback and communications with players			
Analysis of game and players			
Dealing with media / organisations / stakeholders / fans			
Self-management – Personal recovery and post-game regeneration			
Interaction with coaches and support staff			

Coaching Principles

Being a coach is more than just teaching players how to play the game of Rugby. It is a relationship, and as such must be treated with the same respect, and dignity that any relationship deserves.

Develop A Player

The quality of the coaching is critical to the short, and long-term development of the rugby player. It should be continually reviewed, developed, and improved so that not only the process of coaching is developed, but also the coaching behaviour.

There are many ways to play, and different methods of coaching to help players develop their skills. Some coaches put more emphasis on practices designed to build individual skills in isolation, while others focus more on game-like, situational practices aimed at developing better decision-making in the context of a game.

There are two broad approaches to developing players: the first, following the instructions of the coach, is based on practicing, and perfecting individual and collective technical skills like catch and pass, tackle and run lines. This approach is referred to as ***explicit and non-adaptive.***

The second and more player-centred approach prioritises having players practice in a game like situation, in which the players are expected to react to the unexpected, and to link good understanding and decision-making with appropriate technical excellence. It is an ***implicit and adaptive*** approach, depending on the needs of the players at any given moment in their learning how to play effectively.

> ### *Example*
>
> ***Order to Chaos:***
> The old way of coaching was to show a specific drill and then have the players repeat that process again, and again until they mastered the exercise. At the end of the session the coach would then play a conditioned game where he/she would hope that the players put the practiced skill into a game sense environment.... Sometimes it worked......but more often than not it degenerated into a frenzy mediocre end to the session.
>
> ***Chaos to Order:***
> The implicit and adaptive way of coaching approach is to first and foremost let the players show you what they can do, i.e. let them play a conditioned game. The players might surprise you in that they already know the skill that you were about to teach them. Once you have observed them play, the coach can then provide feedback, error correction and skills improvement. Remember that the proven scientific way that we learn, is 10% theory, 20% demonstration and 70% practical applications. A great coaching session is then about improving skill and not just doing a drill again, and again

In summary, approach each and every training session with a clear idea of the objectives and desired output but be open and ready to adapt to coaching opportunities to either accelerate or consolidate learning opportunities.

Coaching Excellence

When you start to consider coaching excellence, you can get lost in the myriad of advice and guidance that there is out in the market. There is even an International Council for Coaching Excellence (ICCE) which is backed by the Association of Summer Olympic International Federation.

The framework covers many great areas of coaching including the framework foundation, the coaching context, coaching roles, coaching competencies, coach education and development, coach certification and recognition and a benefits framework. All great, and wonderful reading material for the academics and process driven coaches that are doing good work in the sport.

There is also an international coach developer framework that covers the role of coach developers, helping the coach to learn development pathways, standards and capabilities, and how to build a coach development system. Again, great reading and some great techniques for developing coaching systems. (see Appendix A for some ideas).

But what makes a great coach? Much the same as what makes a great leader. The question that needs to be asked is can it be modelled…. can it be analysed…. can it be taught, and can it be learned?

So, here is my own personal guide to coaching excellence.

> Do it for the right reason without any consideration of personal gain or benefit. This leads to happiness and joy, everything else you can read in books and learn from the internet. Coaching is my happy place, let it be yours as well.
>
> - *Chris Miles*

Chapter 5:
The Forwards

Chapter Objectives:
In this chapter you will gain knowledge of the following:

- ☑ **The Forwards, their role, and function**
- ☑ **The Scrum**
- ☑ **The Lineout**
- ☑ **Open play**

Overview
Within the game of Rugby Union there are two distinct groups of players. The Forwards, and the Backs.

In the 15-man format of the game there are eight forwards and seven backs, each with a specific set of roles to play during the game. Within the division of Backs and Forwards there are further specialist roles during set piece play such as scrums, lineouts, controlling the pattern of play, and kicking.

Within this chapter you will learn the specific positions of the Forwards, the subunits and the specialist roles in the following positions

- Loose-head Prop (LHP)
- Hooker (H)
- Tight-head Prop (THP)
- Loose-lock (LL)
- Tight-lock (TL)
- Blindside Flanker (BF)

Develop A Player

- Openside Flanker (OF)
- Number Eight (8)

The Forwards, their role, and function

The forwards are made up of eight men split into three distinctive units:

- **The Front Row**
    - Loose-head Prop (No.1)
    - Hooker (No. 2)
    - Tight-head Prop (No. 3)
- **The Second Row**
    - Loose-lock (No. 4)
    - Tight-lock (No. 5)
- **The Back Row**
    - Blindside Flanker (No. 6)
    - Openside Flanker (No. 7)
    - Number Eight (No. 8)

Develop A Player

The Front Row
The front row is made up of three players. Two props', one on the left-hand side of the scrum, known as the Loose-head Prop, and one on the right-hand side, known as the Tight-head Prop, and a Hooker who takes his position in-between the two props'.

Together these three players make up the first of the playing units in the team and form some of the most essential functions in scrum, and lineout restarts.

Loose-Head Prop (No.1) – LHP

The modern game now has the Loose-head Prop (LHP) perform roles traditionally taken on by the Back Row players where they are primarily used as attacking ball carriers in close contact penetration runs, competing at the break-down to both secure ball and put pressure on the opposition, and support line break attacks.

Develop A Player

The role of Loose-head Prop (LHP) is demanding due to the variety of different skills the player needs to learn, however, to compete at the highest level he must learn to master his technique, and his role at Scrums, Lineouts, and in Open play.

Hooker (No.2) - H

The role of the Hooker is one of the most demanding on the rugby pitch because of the variety of different skills a player needs to master. A Hooker must co-ordinate the scrum and direct it because it's his responsibility to hook the ball when it's put into the scrum.

The Hooker also needs to dictate how the lineout unfolds by throwing the ball in from the sidelines to restart the game.

Develop A Player

Both roles are crucial to the success of the team because the scrum and the lineout are the primary sources of possession from a restart in play.

Further, the role of the Hooker in the modern game has developed, and as such the player needs to perform roles traditionally undertaken by the loose forwards by competing at the breakdown and supporting back-line attacks.

Tight-head Prop (No.3) - THP

The Tight-head Prop (THP) is the anchor-man and leads the attack on the opposition scrum. The role is primarily destructive hence the perfect "specimen" is slightly taller than the LHP, extremely well built, solid and difficult to move.

As with the LHP, the THP must learn to work in unison with the entire set of forwards at the scrum to achieve dominance over the opposition pack. The traditional prop was required to have

Develop A Player

the density and bulk to give him power and stability in the scrum, but the modern prop must also be athletic and mobile. That's why the role of the THP has become increasingly more varied and demanding in the modern game.

The Second Row
The second row is made up of two players. The Loose-lock, and the Tight-lock. Together these two players form a vital part of the set piece restarts.

Loose-lock (No. 4) - LL

The Loose-lock (LL) is traditionally one of the key ball winners in many areas of the field, and a specialist both in the lineout and at restarts.

Additionally, the lock is a key component of the scrums providing the power that energises the scrum and so has to work closely with the props to produce the most effective drive possible.

It is also the responsibility of the locks to ensure that the scrum stays stable and binds the props to the hooker as well as providing the platform for the No.8 to add weight and pressure to the scrum.

Tight-lock (No. 5) - TL

The role of the Tight-lock (TL) is very similar to that of the LL in that he is traditionally one of the key ball winners in many areas of the field, and a specialist both in the lineout and at restarts.

The main difference in the names i.e. TL and LL is down to the position they take in the scrum with the Loose-lock (LL) scrummaging between the Loose-head Prop (LHP) and the Hooker (H) and the Tight-lock (TL) scrummaging between the Tight-head Prop (THP) and the Hooker (H). For this reason, the TL tends to be the slightly better scrummager of the two Locks as there is a considerable strategic advantage in supporting the THP putting pressure on the opposition scrum.

Develop A Player

The Back Row
The back row is made up of three players. The Blindside Flanker, Openside Flanker and Number 8. Together this unit of players can be one of the most influential performing not only great attacking options, but also a formidable defensive capability that can have a dramatic impact on the outcome of a game.

Blindside Flanker (No. 6) - BF

The Blindside Flanker (BF) occupies the number 6 shirt on the rugby team and will often be amongst the tallest members of the squad. Many modern Blindside Flankers (BF) are able to cover a number of positions including Tight-lock (TL) or Loose-lock (LL), Openside Flanker (OF), and Number 8 (8) depending on their exact physical attributes. Despite this versatility the position of BF is still a very specialist position, and great Blindside flankers can have more of an impact on the game than most. A modern BF will need to be tall and strong but must also

Develop A Player

be one of the fittest players on the field as he will be expected to play a key role in both attack and defence.

Openside Flanker (No. 7) – OF

The Openside Flanker (OF) occupies the sought-after number seven shirt in a rugby team and will be one the fittest members of the squad due to the vital role he plays. A modern Openside Flanker (OF) is able to cover a number of positions including Blindside Flanker (BF) and Number 8 (8) however having a specialist OF can have a massive impact on the game due to the specific role he plays. A modern OF must make his physical presence felt on the field, which will see him making tackles all over the field, expert in turnovers and gaining hard yards when in position of the ball.

In defence the OF will be expected to be a key defensive lynchpin as well, not just putting in tackle after tackle, but also getting back to his feet to attempt to win turnovers for his team.

Develop A Player

At the breakdown the OF will be expected to be a main ball winner and disrupter of opposition attacks.

Number 8 (No. 8) – 8

The Number 8 (8) player is one of the most influential playing positions on the field. He plays a linking role between the forwards and the backs and as such must be a supreme tactician of the game.

The Number 8 should be capable of putting in massive tackles, making hard yards through contact situations and get involved in open play rugby. The Number 8 (8) will often be one of the most skilful players of the forwards possessing excellent ball handling skills, strong mental strength and even be capable of kicking the ball effectively if required.

Develop A Player

The Number 8 (8) will combine the height of the Blindside Flanker (BF) and the muscular build of a prop. Most modern Number 8's are usually around 190cm tall and weighing around 110Kg. This means that the Number 8 (8) is large enough to be a crucial ball carrying threat to the opposition while at the same time the athleticism to be a jumper in the lineout. It is also vital for the Number 8 to be incredibly fit so that they can get around the field and involve himself in all aspects of the game.

In defence, the Number 8 (8) has an essential role to play putting in substantial defensive tackles to bring down the opposition ball carriers effectively, and the added ability to compete in the ruck to turn over the ball. Setting strong defensive structures is also a vital attribute of the Number 8 (8), being able to defend close around the breakdown as well as knowing defensive structures in the back line.

In attack, the Number 8 (8) has two principal roles in open play attacking rugby:

- **Ball carrier** - The Number 8 (8) must be a strong carrier of the ball with the ability take the ball into contact and retain possession.

- **Playmaker** - The Number 8 (8) must be able to spot weaknesses or mismatches in the opposition defensive structures and be able to exploit these by either taking the ball into contact or setting up players to take advantages of these identified weaknesses.

When the ball is in the opposition half of the field, the (8) will have to decide to either fully commit to the attacking movement or hold back with the fullback and the wingers to form a new attacking movement.

Develop A Player

For further information about each of the forwards; Loose-head prop (LHP), Hooker (H), Tight-head Prop (THP), Loose-lock (LL), Tight-lock (TL), Blindside Flanker (BF), Openside Flanker (OF) and Number 8 (8) a specific book is available for each position.

The Forwards

  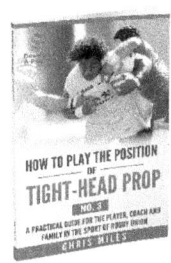

All books are available for sale at **www.developaplayer.com** or through Amazon in a paper-back, kindle or audio format.

A comedic interpretation of the forwards

Props:
These warm, friendly chaps go through life with healthy, albeit often toothless, smiles. But don't let their jolly demeanors fool you: put anything too close to a prop's mouth and you may never see it again.

Hookers: The smallest forward, a hooker is known for his crafty ways and cauliflower ears. Hooking and throwing skills are essential as he is a critical part of any good scrum or lineout. The hooker's job mandates that he has a bald patch on the top of his head, so don't bring it up unless you want your face raked in the next breakdown.

Locks:
Tall and strong, these giants round out the powerhouse that is the tight five. They are known for their strength and athleticism, although not necessarily for their intellect. Most were not actually born slow; it is apparent, however, that years of jamming their heads between the front row's bums have taken a toll on their mental capacities.

Flankers:
These athletic machines have all the speed, talent, and skill of backs, but would rather enjoy the brutality of the scrum than sit idly by and watch the proceedings.

Number 8:
Rounding out the forward pack, this man has no need for a name; rather one refers to him only by number. He may be seen running over opposing forwards, rucking for the otherwise helpless backs, or making booming hits in the open field.

Develop A Player

The Scrum
The official definition of a scrum is "A scrum (short for scrummage) is a method of restarting play in rugby after a stoppage which has been caused by a minor infringement of the Laws (for example, a forward pass or knock on) or the ball becoming unplayable in a ruck or maul. It involves players packing closely together with their heads down and attempting to gain possession of the ball. It is formed by the players who are designated forwards binding together in three rows"

A comedic interpretation of the scrum

"An opportunity for manly men, a chromosome or two short of the intellectual ability to form coherent sentences, to grapple with similar sized men in a wild and blood fuelled contest of physical shenanigans and skulduggery. Neanderthals, some the size of buffaloes, hell bent on pushing, squeezing, biting and cheating their way to dominance over the opposition in a semi organised structure called a scrum, overseen by a referee who has no bloody clue what is going on"

Whether you can relate to the actual description of the scrum, or you prefer to consider the comedic interpretation of what the scrum is, the objective, and purpose is the same, and that is to restart the game with the ball in possession of an attacking side.

Scenarios where a scrum takes place

The full list of the scenarios whereby a scrum can take place are listed here:

Infringement / stoppage	Location of scrum	Who throws in
A knock-on or throw forward, apart from at a lineout.	In the scrum zone at the point closest to the place of infringement.	The non-offending team.
A knock-on or throw forward at a lineout; incorrect throw at a lineout; incorrect quick throw.	15 metres in from the mark of touch.	The non-offending team.
Offside in open play (scrum option).	In the scrum zone at the point closest to where the offending team last played the ball.	The non-offending team.
A penalty or free-kick (scrum option).	In the scrum zone at the point closest to where the infringement took place.	The non-offending team.
The ball is taken into in-goal by the defending team and made dead.	In the scrum zone at the point closest to where the ball was made dead.	The attacking team.
An unplayable	In the scrum zone at	The team last

Develop A Player

tackle or ruck.	the point closest to where the tackle or ruck took place.	moving forward. If neither team was moving forward, the attacking team.
A maul that ends unsuccessfully.	In the scrum zone at the point closest to where the maul ended.	The team not in possession at the start of the maul. If the referee cannot decide which team had possession, the team moving forward before the maul stopped. If neither team was moving forward, the attacking team.
An unplayable maul after kick in open play.	In the scrum zone at the point nearest to place of maul.	The team in possession at the start of the maul.
An incorrect kick-off or restart kick (scrum option).	At the middle point of the half-way line or 22-metre line if the restart kick was a 22 drop-out.	The non-kicking team.
Failure to "use it" at scrum, ruck or maul.	In the scrum zone at the point closest to where the scrum, ruck or maul took	The team not in possession.

	place.	
The ball or ball-carrier touches the referee and either team gains an advantage.	In the scrum zone at the point closest to the incident.	The team that last played the ball.
Stoppage due to injury.	In the scrum zone at the point where the ball was last played.	The team last in possession.
Reset scrum – no infringement.	Where the original scrum took place.	The team originally awarded the scrum.
A penalty attempt at goal not taken within the time limit.	In the scrum zone at the point closest to where the penalty was awarded.	The non-offending team.
A player unable to take a free-kick after a mark within one minute.	In the scrum zone at the point closest to where the free-kick was awarded.	Team of player who was awarded the free-kick.
The referee awards a scrum for any other reason not covered in law.	In the scrum zone at the point closest to the place of stoppage.	The team that was last moving forward or, if neither team was moving forward, the attacking team.

There are however addition key tactical, and strategic considerations in a team being dominant in this part of the game which can lead to physical and mental advantages during the game.

Develop A Player

For example, if a side knows that they will be dominated in a scrum re-start, then they might change their attacking plays to reduce the possibility of an error which would result in a scrum re-start.

Conversely, if a team is dominant in a scrum, then they may choose to be more adventurous in an attacking movement, knowing that even if they knock the ball on, or give a forward pass, it will lead to a scrum, at which point they will be able to re-take control of the ball by pushing the opposition off their restart in the ensuing scrum (referred to as "taking one against the head").

Further, when a side is dominant in a scrum re-start then their side can plan good attacking movements as the opposition must line up at least 10-meters behind the hind most foot of their forwards in the scrum formation as shown below.

Offside lines created from a scrum
This unique field positioning as the result of a scrum re-start, and creation of the off-side lines, means that the side in possession of the ball after the scrum is over is at a significant advantage to play great attacking moves through the back line.

Develop A Player

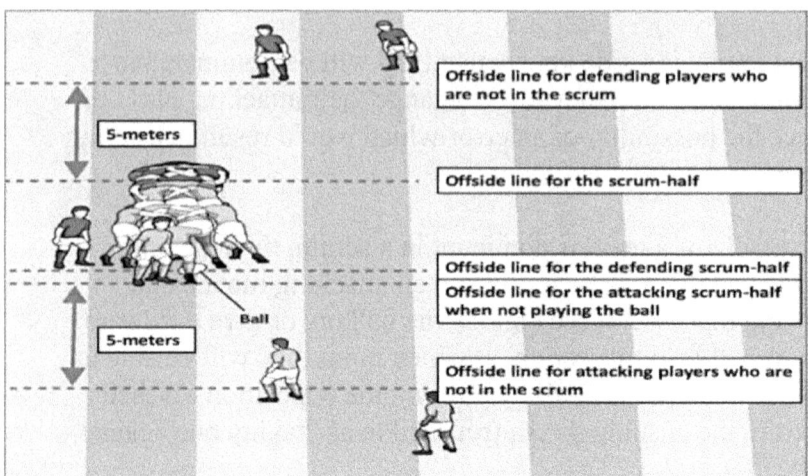

However, before the backs can get that opportunity to play, the forwards need to dominate the scrum, win the ball, and provide the platform from which to attack.

Develop A Player

The formation of a scrum

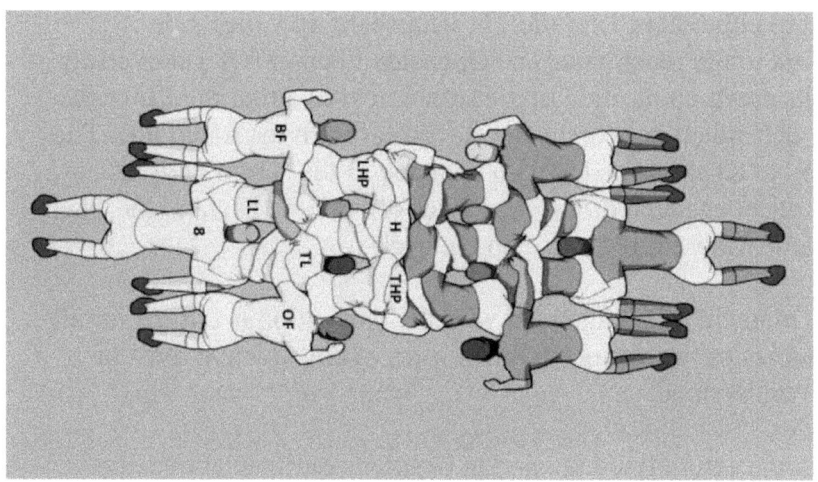

The below illustration shows the formation of a full 8-man scrum

Each of the front row players have a specific role. The Loose-head Prop (LHP) packs down on the left-hand side of the scrum. He engages with his opposite number with his right shoulder only. The Hooker (H) is also in the front row between the LHP and the Tight-head Prop (THP). The THP packs down on the right-hand side of the scrum. He engages with his opposite number with both his left and right shoulder. Together these three players make up the front row unit.

The Loose Lock (LL) packs down in the scrum on the left-hand side. He binds onto the Tight-lock (TL) with his right arm, and engages with both shoulders on the backsides of both the LHP and the H. The Tight-lock (TL) binds onto the LL with his left arm and engages both shoulders on the backsides of both the H and the THP. Together these two players make up the second-row unit.

Develop A Player

The Blindside Flanker (BF) packs down on the side of the scrum next to either the LL or the TL, dependant on which side is closest to the touch line. The Openside Flanker (OL) conversely packs down on the side of the scrum next to either the LL or the TL, dependant on which side is furthest from the touch line. The Number 8 (8) backs down on the back of the scrum with his shoulders engaged on the backsides of both the LL, and the TL. Together these three make up the back-row unit.

The moment of engagement with the opposition is critical for all members of the scrum, so the process of engagement must be well understood.

With the scrum lined up, and in positions outlined above, the referee will call:

- "**Crouch!**", instructing front row to do so, then
- "**Bind!**", instructing the opposition props to grab onto the back/shoulder of each other's jersey, and then
- "**Set!**", indicating that the front rows can come together when ready

The referee's instruction allows the props to prepare for the moment of contact. It is vital for all members of the scrum to work in harmony to put pressure on the opposition pack.

For further, and more detailed information on the specific roles of each position, including the dark arts of scrummaging play there are additional reading resources who wish to perfect their skills in this area of play.

Develop A Player

The Lineout
The official definition of a lineout is "The lineout is a means of restarting play after the ball has gone into touch (off the field of play at the side). When this happens play stops and is restarted with a lineout. Forwards from the two teams form two close parallel lines (1 metre apart) and a player throws in the ball from outside the field of play.

A comedic interpretation of the lineout

"When a member of either side has not been able to play within the boundaries of the playing field, or worse a back has kicked it out of the field of play, the ball is given to the forwards to re-start the game. They do this by throwing the ball in from the sideline while at this time the second rows leap into the air like majestic salmon swimming upstream supported by the brutish strength of the props to get them even higher, The back row sometimes get involved but mainly they focus on hatching plans of skulduggery and illegal running lines in an attempt to get close enough to the opposition outside half to wipe the mascara off his handsome face."

Develop A Player

Scenarios where a lineout takes place

Where the game is restarted with a lineout and which team throws in is determined as follows:

Event	Location of the mark of touch	Who throws in
The ball-carrier goes into touch.	Where the player touches the touchline or the ground beyond it.	The opposition.
A player unintentionally knocks, passes or throws the ball into touch.	Where the ball reaches the touchline.	The opposition.
A player, who is in touch, catches or picks up a ball which has reached the plane of touch.	Where the ball reached the plane of touch.	The team of the player who caught or picked up the ball.
A player, who is in touch, catches or picks up a ball which has not reached the plane of touch.	Where that player is standing.	The opposition.

Develop A Player

For whatever reason, and there are many more than the main ones identified in the previous table, the game needs to be re-started from the sideline with a lineout.

Over the years, both forwards and backs have participated in the lineout, however in the modern game it is primarily the forwards who are tasked with this aspect of the game with the Hooker (H) throwing the ball in.

Offside lines created from a lineout
There are a multitude of technical aspects to the lineout which we will cover here, however a key difference between a scrum and a lineout is the offside line. In a scum the offside line is 5m from the back of the scrum, whereas the offside line is 10m back from where the lineout takes place.

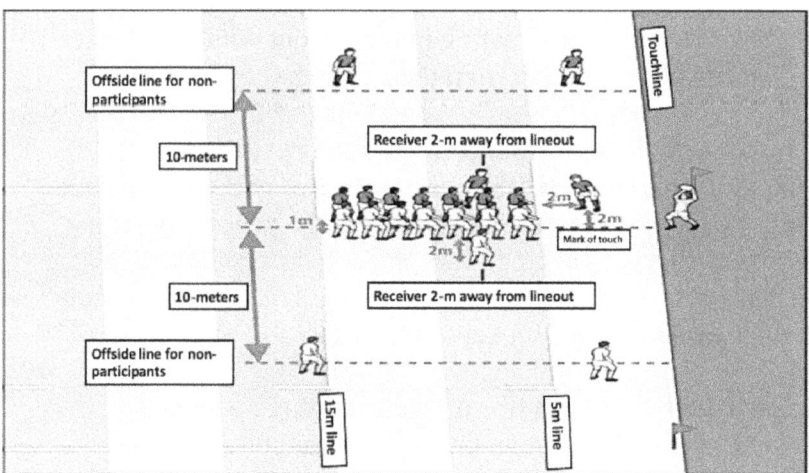

Lineout options
There are numerous combinations of lifters', jumpers, trick moves and switches that can be used during the lineout restart however the objectives are the same:

Develop A Player

- to secure the ball on your own throw, and set up a back-line attack or
- to secure the ball, and to set up a forward attack.

At the lineout At least two players from each team must form a lineout, with a maximum of thirteen. There are however three kinds of lineout configurations that the majority of teams use in the modern game:

- **8-man lineout** – Both props, both locks and the backrow all participate in the lineout with the Hooker throwing the ball in from the side-line.
- **5-man lineout** – Both props, both locks and one member of the backrow participating in the lineout with the Hooker throwing the ball in from the sideline.
- **3-man lineout** – One prop, one lock and one member of the backrow participating in the lineout with the Hooker throwing the ball in from the sideline.

The reason why these lineout configurations exist is because of the jumping options they offer for the Hooker to throw too. Due to the introduction of lifting in the lineout the concept of lifting pods was introduced whereby two players, one front, and one behind are able to support the jumper reach higher in the lineout making it easier for the Hooker to throw too.

Therefore, with an 8-man lineout there are three potential jumping Pod's, with a 5-man lineout there are two potential jumping pods, and with a 3-man lineout there is one potential jumping pod.

Develop A Player

To start from the basic set up there are three primary jumping spots in the lineout:

- **Pod 1 (front)** – this is a throw to the front of the lineout. The throw is primarily a fast throw directly to the anticipated point in the air where the Pod 1 jumper will reach. In a conventional 8-man lineout the Loose-lock (LL) normally jumps at the front. He is supported by the Loose-head Prop (LHP) in front of him, and the Tight-head Prop (THP) from behind.

Develop A Player

Pod 1 (front) jump

- **Pod 2 (middle)** – this is a throw to the middle of the lineout. The throw can either be a direct fast throw or a weighted lob to the anticipated point in the air where the Pod 2 jumper will reach. In a conventional 8-man lineout the Tight-lock (TL) normally jumps at the middle. He is supported by the Tight-head Prop (THP) in front of him, and the Blindside Flanker (BF) from behind

Pod 2 (middle) jump

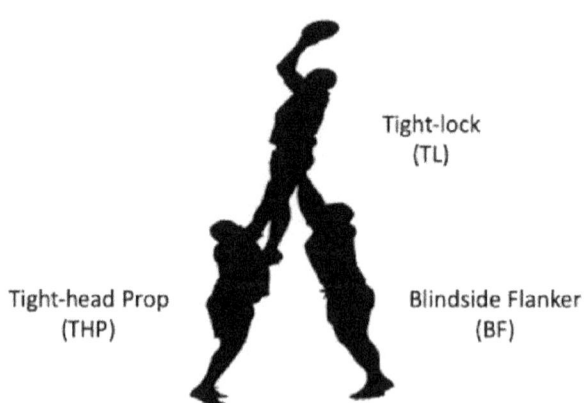

Develop A Player

- **Pod 3 (back)** - this is a throw to the back of the lineout which is primarily a weighted lob to the anticipated point in the air where the Pod 3 jumper will reach. In a conventional 8-man lineout the Openside Flanker (OF) normally jumps at the back. He is supported by the Blindside Flanker (BF) in front of him, and the Number 8 (8) from behind.

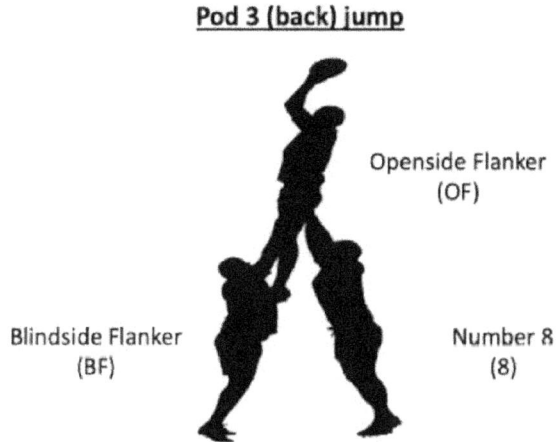

Pod 3 (back) jump

Lineout Calls

Once the lineout positions have been decided, and the lifting pods agreed upon, the next thing to consider are the calls to decide which jumping pod the ball should be thrown too in a live game of rugby.

The reason for this is to allow the side throwing in the ball the opportunity to assess the way the opposition is setting up against them, assess, and then adjust the jumping position to increase the probability of them being able to win the ball cleanly in the lineout and commence an attacking movement.

Develop A Player

As you can imagine there are numerous options that can be used to signal to all the players in the lineout where the ball will be thrown too, however all have a pattern which can be adapted specific to the desires of each team. Some of the more common methods are identified below.

- **Jack, Queen, King** – Before the lineout commences, one of the players calls out a word beginning with "*J*"; "*A*"; "*C*", or "*K*". this would indicate that the ball will be thrown to the ***front***.

   Similarly, any word beginning with "*Q*"; "*U*"; "*E*", or "*N*" will be a throw to the ***middle***.

   Finally, any word beginning with "*K*"; "*I*"; "*N*"; "*G*" will be a throw to the ***back***

   > *Example*: "*Apple*… 2… 4… 6…" = ***Front*** (other numbers are added to try and hide the code).

- **Drinks, Country, Colour** – Before the lineout commences, one of the players calls a drink, e.g. "*milk*" this would indicate that the ball will be thrown to the ***front***.

   Similarly, any country e.g. "*Australia*" will be a throw to the ***middle***.

   Finally, any colour e.g. "*Black*" will be a throw to the ***back***

   > *Example*: "27… Australia… 32…" = ***Middle*** (other numbers are added to try and hide the code).

Develop A Player

- **Scrum half hand position** – This tactic can be quite interesting as there are no actual calls once the lineout is formed. If the scrum half has his *hands on his knees,* then the ball will be thrown to the *front*

    Similarly, if the scrum half has his *hands on his hips*, then the ball will be a throw to the *middle*.

    Finally, if the scrum half has his *hands not touching anything*, then the ball will be a throw to the *back*.

> The combinations are almost endless, e.g. *123… Australia* could be to the *front going forward*, and *Black ….456* could be to the *back going backwards*, however using these example blueprints will allow the coach to develop unique calls for his/her side.

Develop A Player

Chapter 6:

The Backs

Chapter Objectives:
In this chapter you will gain knowledge of the following:

- ☑ **The Backs, their role, and function**
- ☑ **Attacking moves by the backs**
- ☑ **Defensive structures by the backs**

Overview
Within the game of Rugby Union there are two distinct groups of players. The Forwards, and the Backs.

In the 15-man format of the game there are eight forwards and seven backs, each with a specific set of roles to play during the game.

Within this chapter you will learn the specific positions of the backs, the subunits and the specialist roles in the following positions

- Scrum-half (SH)
- Outside-half (OH)
- Inside Centre (IC)
- Outside Centre (OC)
- Blindside Winger (BW)
- Openside Winger (OW)
- Fullback (F)

Develop A Player

The Backs, their role, and function
The backs are made up of seven men split into three distinctive units:

- **Half-backs**
    o Scrum-half (SH)
    o Outside-half (OH)

- **Inside Backs**
    o Inside Centre (IC)
    o Outside Centre (OC)

- **Outside Backs**
    o Blindside Winger (BW)
    o Openside Winger (OW)
    o Fullback (F)

Develop A Player

The Half Backs
The half-backs are the playmaker of the game, linking the forward to the inside and outside backs in a variety of passing and kicking tactics in the game.

Scrum-half (No. 9) - SH

The Scrum-half (SH) is one of the key players in the team. He is at the centre of all that happens and the link between the forwards and the backs, the coordinator of the game and the player who can most influence the pace of the game. He is usually the player in deciding the calls at lineout and scrums, an accurate passer of the ball and a good kicker, a good tackler, quick off the mark, an evasive runner, a motivator, a decision maker, a reader of the game and a tactician

The Scrum-half (SH) must have good judgment and have fast reactions to exploit an attacking opportunity when it presents itself in a game. Kicking is also an essential part of the SH's

Develop A Player

game and therefore must be superb at kicking off both the left and the right foot.

In attack, a high work-rate is essential as the SH needs to get to every single breakdown and therefore must continuously communicate between the forwards and the backs.

Although the SH is often the smallest player on the pitch, he is also amongst one of the most tenacious. A good SH needs to have high on-field leadership skills to help manage his team's play and be able to influence the referee without becoming a nuisance!

The SH must also be amongst the fittest players on the pitch as they will need to run from ruck to ruck to distribute the ball, thus keeping the attacking movement going. The SH will have one of the most rounded skill sets on the field able to kick, tackle and pass well on either side with all three of these skill sets being regularly tested throughout a match.

The SH is a crucial leader of the pack and must be the eyes of their forwards during rucks and scrums making decisions for them and distributing them around the field in both attack and defence.

The SH has a variety of roles to play while the ball is in open play. One of their key roles is the distribution of the ball from the base of the ruck. After the forwards have secured the ball, the SH will pick the ball up from the base of the breakdown to either recycle it through his forwards or distribute it out to his backs to run a play. In defensive rucks, the SH will usually stand behind the ruck ready to defend against any player who may attempt to run around the sides and break through the first defensive line.

Develop A Player

The SH may also opt to kick the ball either to try to gain territory or by utilising the box kick to allow his team to attempt to reclaim the ball after it is kicked into the air. As a final alternative, the SH may decide to run the ball themselves if they feel a gap has opened up in the opposition defensive line which would allow them to dart through.

Both in attack and defence, the SH must organise their teams' forwards, distributing them around the field to either create an opening in attack or to counter any potential opposition moves

Outside-half (No.10) – OH

The Outside-half (OH) is often considered the go-to man on the field. The person in this position controls the attack and dictates how a team decides to penetrate an opposition's defence. The Outside-half (OH) is often used as the vital orchestrator of a

Develop A Player

defensive system. Their primary job in defence is to produce the line speed of a defensive line to cut down space from the opposition, in turn forcing the attack to execute under pressure.

The role of an Outside-half (OH) varies from team to team. However, a good OH who inspires to excel in their position will have a substantial skill set and can produce high-level skills under pressure.

An OH should be continually looking to make ground and identify weaknesses in an opposition's defence. A great OH can locate the space in the defence and consistently make the best decisions on how to exploit the shortcomings of the opposition. Team strategy and game plans are often executed through the OH who plays a pivotal role in adapting to the game as it unfolds as well as in initiating patterns and plays from the set piece.

This position requires the highest degree of talent in the execution of skills such as game management, leadership, distribution, and kicking.

Develop A Player

The Inside Backs

The inside backs' is a paring of the inside Centre (IC) and the Outside Centre (OC). These two ball players can be the most influential on the backline attack plays and hence need to be great tacticians and highly skilled in the discipline of catch and pass, kicking and strong running.

Inside Centre (No.12) – IC

Although the Inside Centre (IC) and Outside Centre's (OC) roles are very similar, there are some fundamental differences that mean players specialise in one of the two positions, although typically, a player should feel comfortable playing at Inside Centre (IC) or Outside Centre (OC).

The Inside Centre (IC) is generally the larger of the pair as they are a critical defensive lynchpin in the team's midfield so must be capable of tackling even the largest of opponents.

Develop A Player

An IC should possess many of the skills of an Outside-half (OH) and therefore be comfortable acting as a first receiver should the Outside-half (OH) be unable to receive the ball from a set piece move or an open play situation.

A good IC should have excellent leadership skills, able to help their OH organise the team around them in both attack and defence. He should be a good decision maker as he is likely to play the second receiver role in the team so must feel comfortable deciding whether to run the ball, kick it or distribute it out to the Outside Centre (OC).

If the IC is an active playmaker, then the OC is more likely to be a dynamic runner during the game, choosing to run off the pass from the IC and taking it past the gain-line. If the IC is a stronger runner, then the OC may instead act as more of a play-maker, latching onto the IC's off-loads and looking to distribute the ball out to the wings.

Modern OC's generally have quite a large build and should look like they would be comfortable playing in the back row of the scrum. The IC will line up just outside the OH in their team's formations, although if they are comfortable playing the role of the first receiver they may find themselves lining up on the opposite side of the play to the OH to offer the SH multiple passing options from the scrum.

Develop A Player

Outside Centre (No.13) – OC

Although the Outside Centre (OC) is commonly slightly smaller in build than the Inside Centre (IC), they are generally the more effective tackler of the two due to the size of the field they need to cover as well as the vital role they play in being able to take on ball runners who are running at him from depth at pace.

Although not crucial it is also of benefit if the Outside Centre (OC) feels comfortable kicking the ball out of hand. While they will rarely need to kick the ball, it is beneficial if they can provide an additional kicking option in defence to alleviate any pressure their team may be under.

The Outside Centre (OC) should also have good passing technique and be comfortable passing off either hand and able to have the vision of knowing when to put his team's winger into space to run in the try.

Develop A Player

The two critical roles for an OC are to act as an additional play-maker in the back-line attack and creating a solid defensive line that is difficult for the opposition to breach.

The two centres' must be comfortable tackling even the biggest of the opposition's forwards. In addition to making significant tackles and applying pressure to the oppositions ball carriers, the OC will often be expected to act as an additional back-row forward at the breakdown competing for the ball and attempting to turn over the oppositions ball.

The Outside Backs
The outside backs are made up of the three positions Blindside Winger (BW), Openside Winger (OW), and Fullback (F). They take up the positions on the far left and far right of the field of play. They are one of the most effective positions for scoring as they are normally the fastest plays on the field in attack, and the last line of defence.

Blindside Winger (No.11) – BF

Develop A Player

A winger in rugby will be amongst one of the fastest players on the pitch while also having a well-round skill set. Although being out on the wing, they may not be as heavily involved in the action as some of the other players on the pitch they still have an essential role to play in both attack and defence.

A winger will usually be light on their feet and confident running with the ball in hand while taking on the opposition one-on-one.

A winger may also have to put in some of the most critical tackles on the pitch as if they are beaten on the outside then it is unlikely the oppositions line breaker will be caught before reaching the try-line.

The decision on which side a winger will play depends on their particular strengths. A right-handed and right-footed winger is likely to play for the right winger and vice versa for left wingers. This is because a winger is usually the last man before the ball reaches touch so is more likely to have to play the ball back inside as there is unlikely to be someone stood outside of them.

Also, a predominantly right-footed winger is likely to step off their right foot so will want their stronger leg on the outside to step inside players. While the differences between left and right wingers may only be very subtle, the small margins can make a big difference.

Taking consideration of the strengths and weakness of the winger will therefore help determine which side of the field each plays' on. The terminology of Blindside Winger (BW) and Openside Winger (OW) is therefore somewhat irrelevant in the modern game as both should be equally capable.

Develop A Player

A winger should try to hug to the touchline, waiting for the ball to be distributed out through the centres for an opening. Once the ball comes out to the winger, they will look to take the ball to the opposition, keeping it in hand and looking to break through the defensive line.

Top wingers should also feel comfortable putting boot to ball and kicking down field should an opportunity present itself. As one of the fastest members of the team, the winger will usually be expected to chase his own kick and look to either reclaim the ball or put pressure on the opposition catcher.

In defence, a winger will usually be expected to defend the far side of the pitch hugging the touchline and is most likely to have to tackle the opposition winger. If the ball is in the opposition's half, the winger will usually hold back ready to claim any long clearance kicks by the opposition to relieve pressure.

Openside Winger (No.14) – OW

Develop A Player

An Openside Winger (OW) in rugby will be amongst one of the fastest players on the pitch while also having a well-round skill set. All the other attributes, competencies, and decision-making skills needed to play OW are the same as the Blindside Winger (BW).

Fullback (No.15) - F

Develop A Player

A great Fullback (F) will be an excellent play-maker, being able to control the back-line in both attack and defence.

He will be ready to kick the ball accurately and over great distances while possessing the speed to cover large areas quickly and with purpose.

A Fullback (F) should feel comfortable filling in at Outside-half (OH) or on the wing should his team require it.

The Fullback (F) needs to understand the strategies and tactics of both forward and back play to contribute fully to the game in this crucial position.

The F will usually be a very similar build to the wingers – tall and slim but with plenty of lean muscle power. This physical build allows him to be quick across the field while also being able to make significant last-ditch tackles and even leap into the air to successfully compete for high kicks.

The F is both the last line of defence and a key point of attack in his team so he must be equally comfortable running with the ball in hand or making the crucial try-saving tackle while in defence.

It is often common for an aspiring Outside-halve (OH) to learn their trade at Fullback (F) where they must put to use all of the kicking types, passing and running skills necessary to make it as a top player.

In defence, the role performed by the Fullback (F) is particularly essential. The F will typically hang back behind his own back-line and positioned himself in the middle of the field ready to collect any ball kicked over the top. Once he has caught the kick, the F must then decide whether to run the ball back or to kick it back to gain territory. Should the F kick the ball, he needs

Develop A Player

to be prepared to chase it up the field to play the rest of his team onside.

In attack, the F should be able to scan the game scenario and decide whether to run the ball at the opposition or if his team is pinned back in their own half, then the F may determine that a kicking option is best to get his team out of trouble.
Although the F may at first appear to be on the peripheries of his team, they will be heavily involved in the game and will have their hands on the ball more often than not. They must, therefore, feel comfortable having their hands on the ball in any situation while also being capable of efficiently reading the play.

For further information about each of the backs; Scrum-half (SH), Outside-half (OH), Inside Centre (IC), Outside Centre (OC), Blindside Winger (BW), Openside Winger (OW) and Fullback (F) a specific book is available for each position.

The Backs

Develop A Player

Attacking moves by the backs
When you start to consider the multiple and varied options there are in a coming up with back line attack patterns a coach could start to get giddy over all the diabolic, devious, and down-right genius moves that can be conceived and brought to bare of an unsuspected opposition.

Straight line running, unders', overs', switch backs, scissor moves, dummy scissor moves, miss one, miss two, out the back, over the top, along the ground, deep, wide, aerial bombs…. the list goes on, and on of moves, coded names given to pre-defined attack patters, secret, and double secret moves…. a poor coach could almost go insane over the smorgasbord board of attack options and combinations.

There are however, a few universal, and basic principles that a developing coach can follow to develop their own unique attacking moves and patterns.

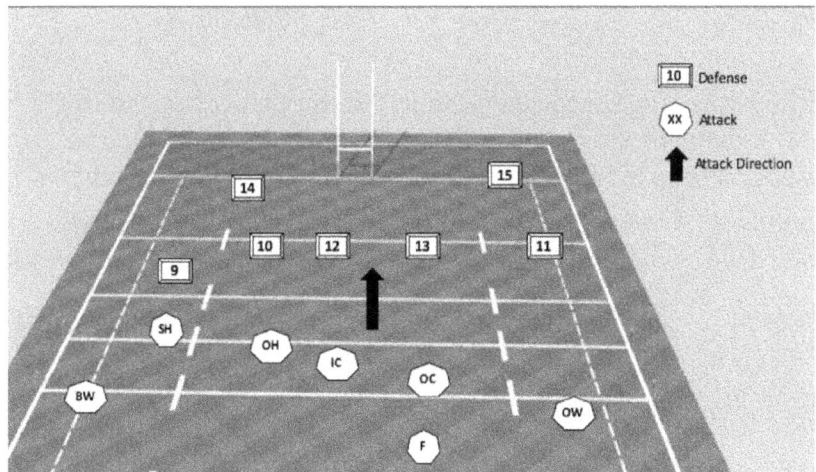

Develop A Player

Attacking principal 1- Create attack space

In the example below the attacking Inside Centre (IC) has run up and left, drawing the opposition 12 in the same direction. Additionally, the Outside Centre (OC) has run forward, and right, drawing the opposition 13 in the same direction. This has left an attack space which the Fullback (F) can run into.

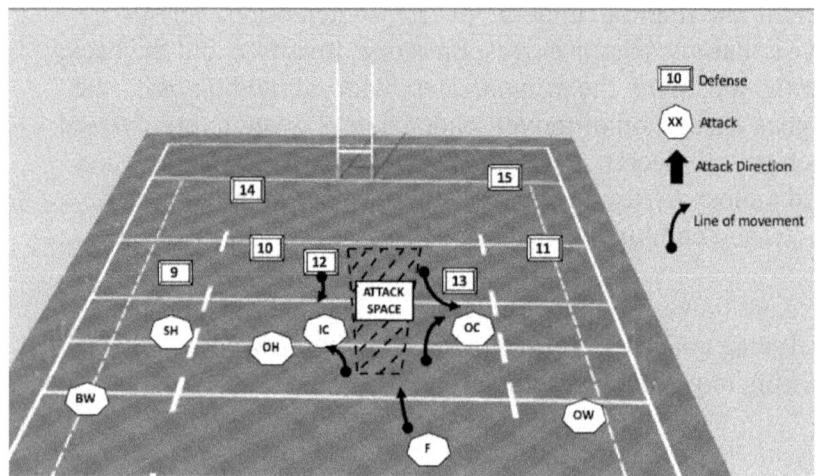

Creating attacking space can be achieved through various means however they all rely on the opposition players moving out of a defensive structure in some way so as to leave a space for other attacking players to run into and cross the gain line thus setting up a scoring opportunity for his/her team mates.

Develop A Player

Attacking principal 2 – Create overloads

In the example below the Inside Centre (IC) has held his opposite number, so as the Outside Centre (OC). At the same time the Fullback (F) has run outside the OC. This movement has resulted in two attacking players i.e. the Fullback (F) and the Openside Winger (OW) against on opposition 11.

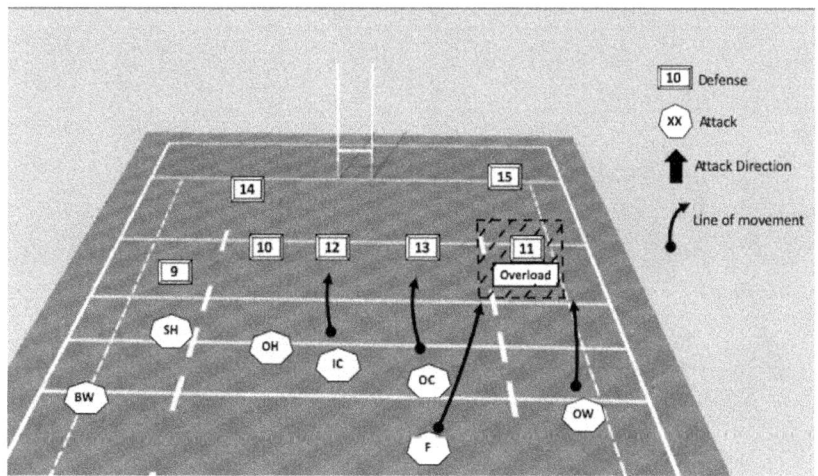

Wherever there are more attacking players than there are defending players an overload has occurred. Once this situation has been achieved it is then down to the competencies of the players to seize and capitalise on the scoring opportunity.

Develop A Player

Attacking principal 3 – Create mismatches

In the example the Blindside Winger (BW) is attacking up the left-hand side of the pitch. By doing so it is hoped that the speed, agility, and skill of the BW is better than that of the defending 9 thereby allowing the BW to get passed the defending 9 and capitalise on the scoring opportunity.

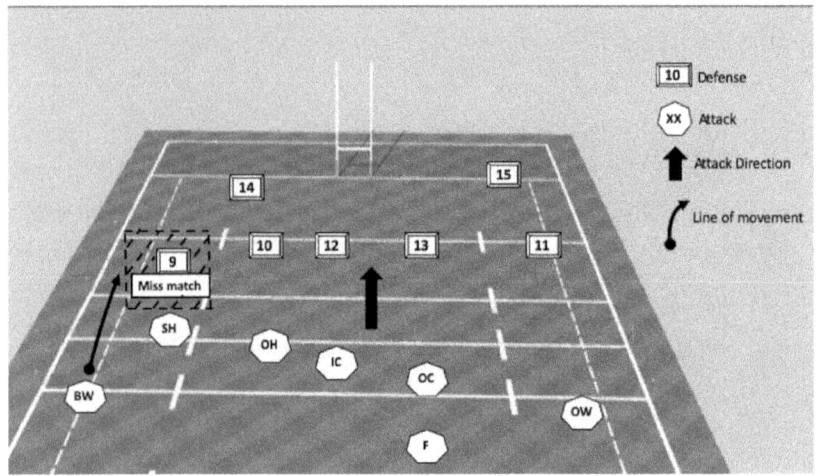

Miss-matches relay a lot on the playing competencies of the individual player. Mismatches, however, are not limited to backs versus backs. Miss matches can be orchestrated where stronger, players such as props and locks are attacking against outside backs, or faster more mobile backs are attacking against heavier and slower forwards.

Defensive structures by the backs

With the evolution of more sophisticated attack moves and patterns, the defensive structures of the backs as also evolved. In fact, the defensive work of most teams in the modern game of rugby is so good that we now see upwards of fifteen phases of rugby without giving any significant territorial loss in terms of gain line advancement by an attacking team.

There are many reasons for this including better communications, better speed, fitness and endurance, tactical awareness of opposition intentions in terms of generating space, overloads or miss-matches, but by far the advancement in defensive structures has been the influence of defensive policies from Rugby League.

For those unfamiliar with the sport of Rugby League it is a modified version of Rugby Union first played on August 29th, 1895 when clubs in the North of England broke away from the Rugby Football Union (RFU) with Rugby Union remained an amateur sport until the summer of 1995, 100-years later. The game is still played on the same size field but with 13-players and more structured rules. In summary each side has 6-opportunities to run with the ball to try and score a try, if they are not successful in that attempt then they must turn the ball over to the opposition and given them an opportunity to score.

There are a lot more rules to the format of Rugby League however in principal that's the game. Therefore, as you can appreciate the defensive work needs to be excellent to not just stop one hard attacking run, but to stop six, one after another has meant that the defensive work needs to be exceptional. Those same defensive disciplines have now found their way into the game of Rugby Union, and these are the basic attack principals that can be considered when developing more advanced policies for a team.

Develop A Player

Defence principal 1 – Man on Man Marking

Man-on-man marking relies heavily on individual skills being the same or if not better than your opposition. A straight-line defence moves up together to try and stop any attack by the opposition team.

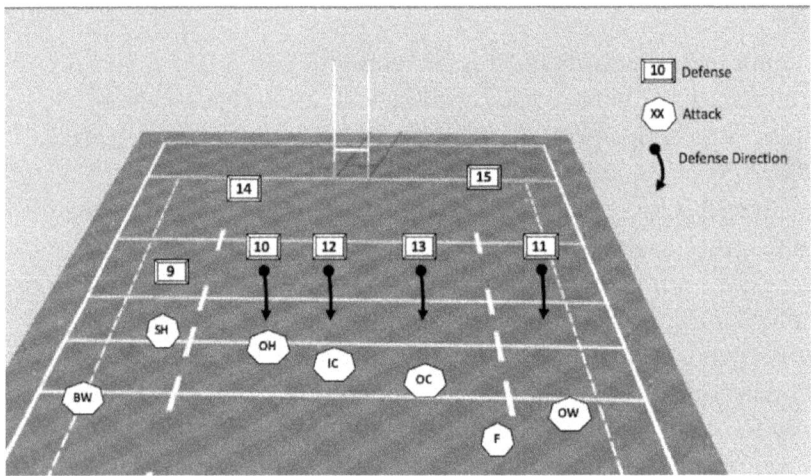

This kind of defence works well against opposition teams that are not very creative in their attacking competencies and have few or no attacking variations.

Develop A Player

Defence principal 2 – Umbrella

The defending team has all players' 10, 12, 13 and 14 running up at a different pace. This relies on great communications between all the players, and simultaneous timing to create the defensive shape as identified in the below diagram

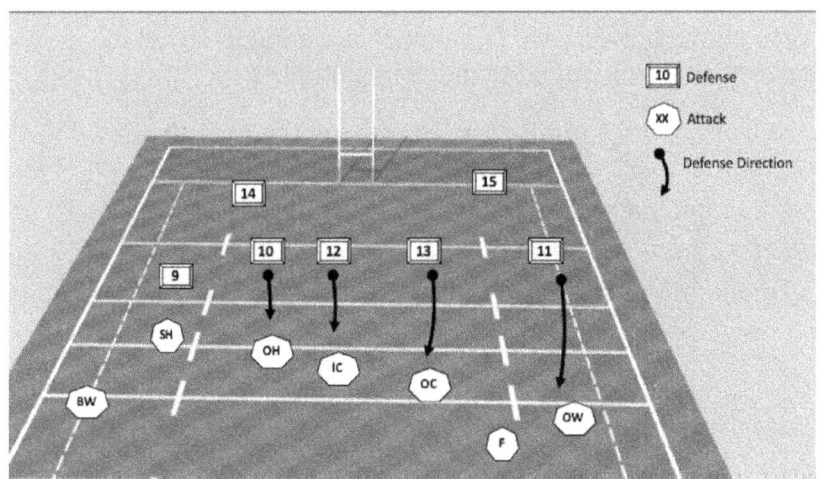

The is shape is called an umbrella defence and is used to prevent the attacking team moving the ball quickly to their outside backs i.e. Openside Winger (OW) or Fullback (F).

This defensive pattern would be used when an attacking team has good attacking outside backs, and hence the objective is to prevent the ball being passed to those players.

Develop A Player

Defence principal 3 – Drift

The defending team has all players' 10, 12, 13 and 14 running up at a same pace in a two directional way. First, they go forward, and then they push to the outside thus forcing the attacking players to pass to the outside player and resist coming back the other way. This relies on great communications between all the players, and simultaneous timing to create the defensive drift as identified in the diagram below.

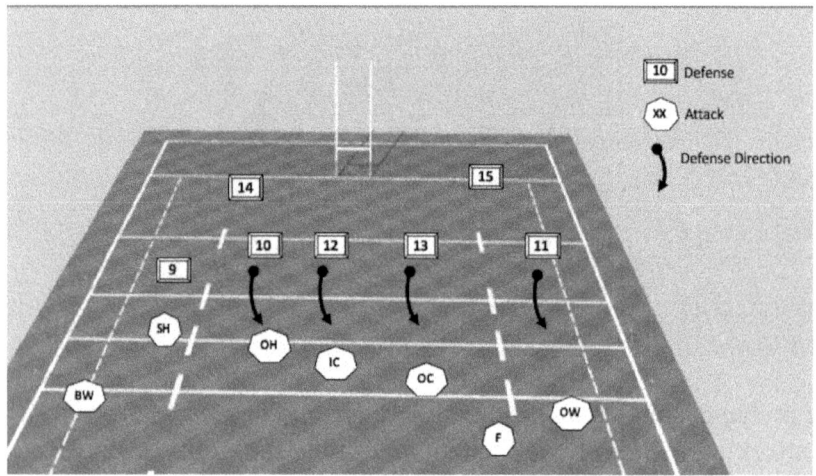

This kind of defensive patter would be used against opposition teams that have a strong Inside Centre (IC) or good back row players who would be able to maintain continuity of the attacking play. By adopting these patterns forces the attacking team to move the ball quicker to the outside backs

Develop A Player

Defence principal 4 – Smother

The defending team has all players' 10, 12, 13 and 14 running up at a same pace in a two directional way. First, they go forward, and then they push to the inside thus forcing the attacking players to pass to the inside backs i.e. Inside Centre (IC) and Outside Centre (OC). This relies on great communications between all the players, and simultaneous timing to create the smother defensive structure as identified in the diagram below.

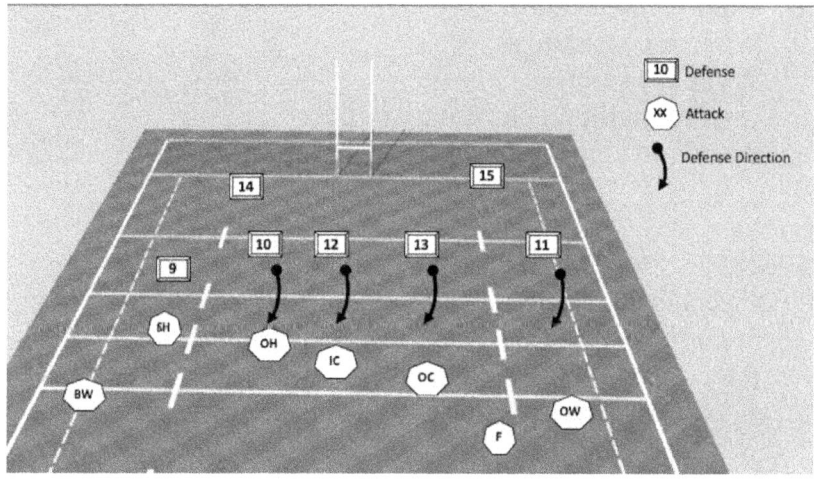

This kind of defensive patter would be used against opposition teams that have strong outside backs i.e. Outside Wingers (OW) or Fullbacks (F) who have great speed and pace. By adopting this pattern, it forces the attacking team to keep the ball closer into the forwards.

Chapter 7:
Open play Rugby

Chapter Objectives:
In this chapter you will gain knowledge of the following:

- ☑ Field segmentation
- ☑ What are structures
- ☑ What are shapes
- ☑ How to maintain continuity in play
- ☑ Pros' and Cons' of structure v heads up Rugby

Overview
As a coach progresses from coaching junior players to more senior players there is a need to start teaching players structures and shapes. The reason for this is because structures give players a focus and a plan of action they can rely upon when defences do not offer easy opportunities to exploit.

Field Segmentation
To develop attacking shapes, and structures the coach first needs to analyse the field of play in some detail, and also more fully understand the capabilities of the players' so effective strategies and tactics can be developed.

Develop A Player

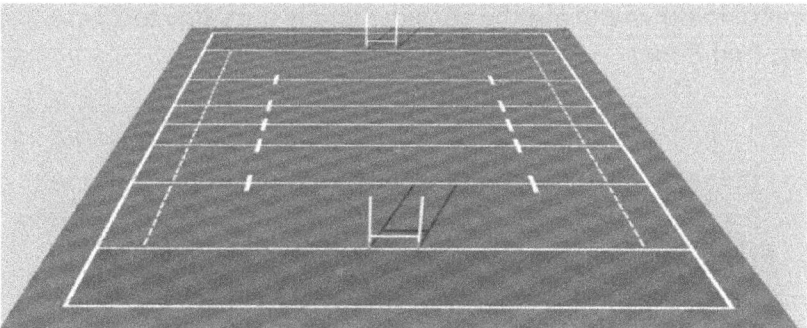

A rugby field can be thought of as multiple channels running end to end and zones running from sideline to sideline.

The simplest of channels can be understood from the following with three channels of attack: Wide Left, Centre field and wide right.

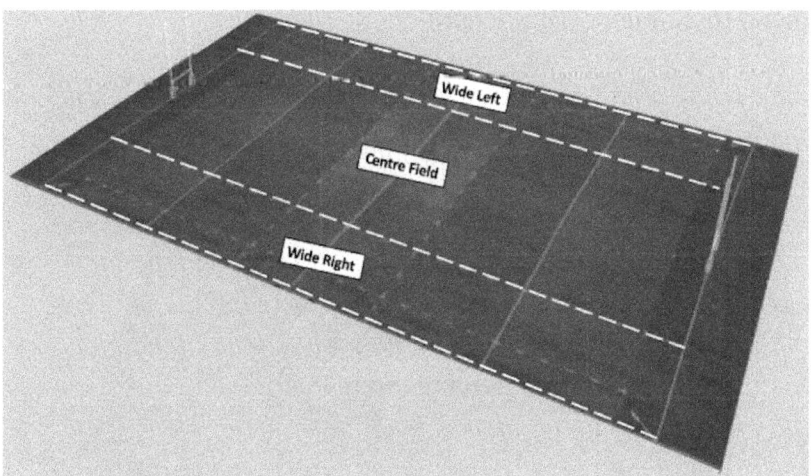

Develop A Player

Three basic zones can also be considered: Own try line to 22-meter; (red Zone)

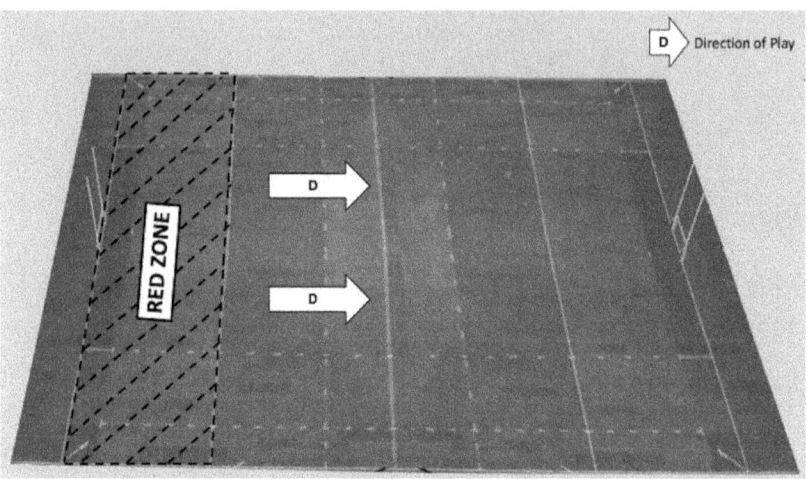

22-meter to 22-meter (Blue Zone)

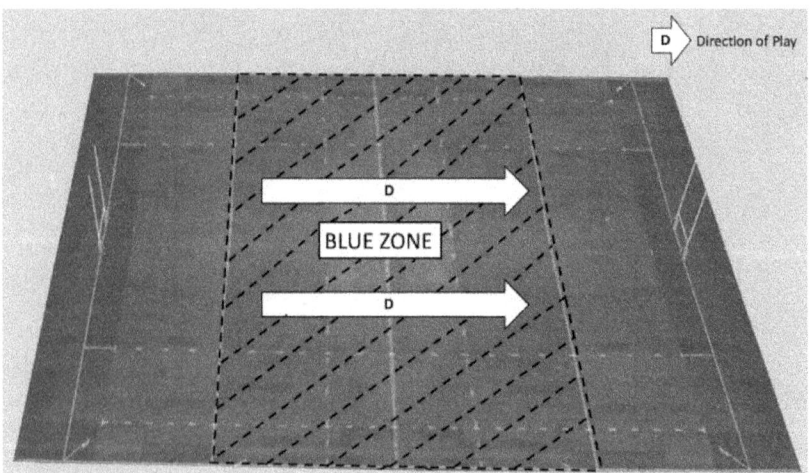

Develop A Player

And 22-meter to opposition try line (Green Zone).

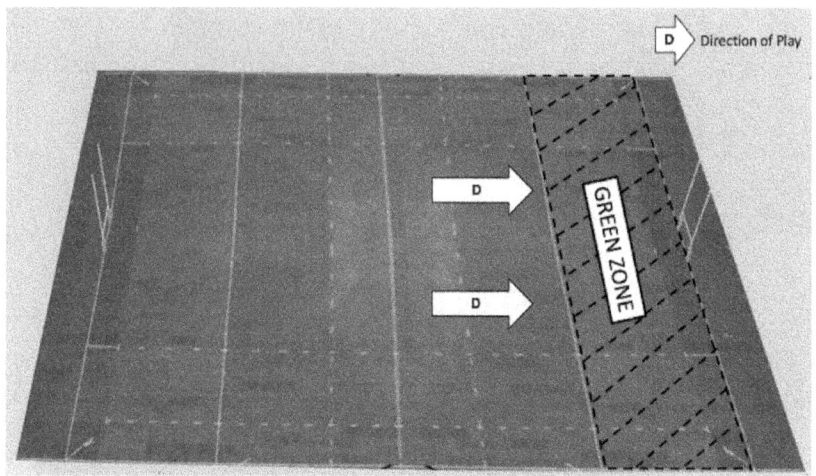

Therefore, with a basic understanding of field segmentation and playing zones, structured play, and attacking shapes can be developed to move through the zones of the field.

Structures
A structure of play can be thought of as a way to move through the zones of the field with the two concepts of 'Same-way' and 'rewind' as shown in the below illustration starting from a lineout:

Develop A Player

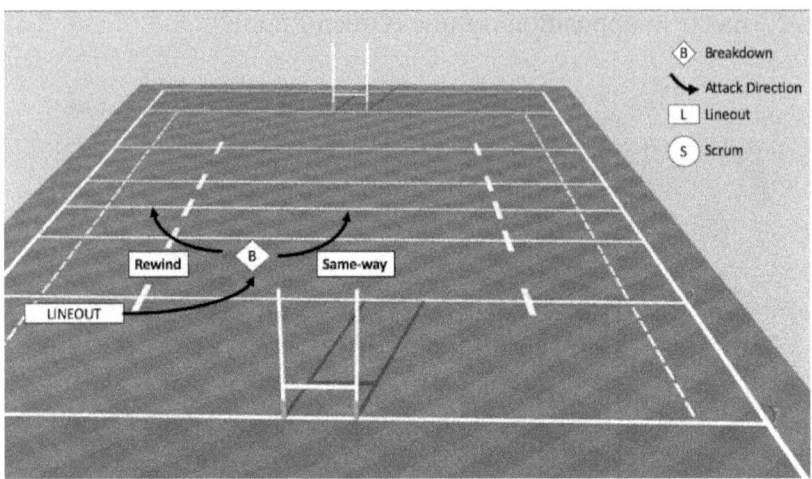

An attacking structure that keeps going the same way is commonly referred to as an exhaust pattern which has the attacking time continuing to attack from left to right or right to left.

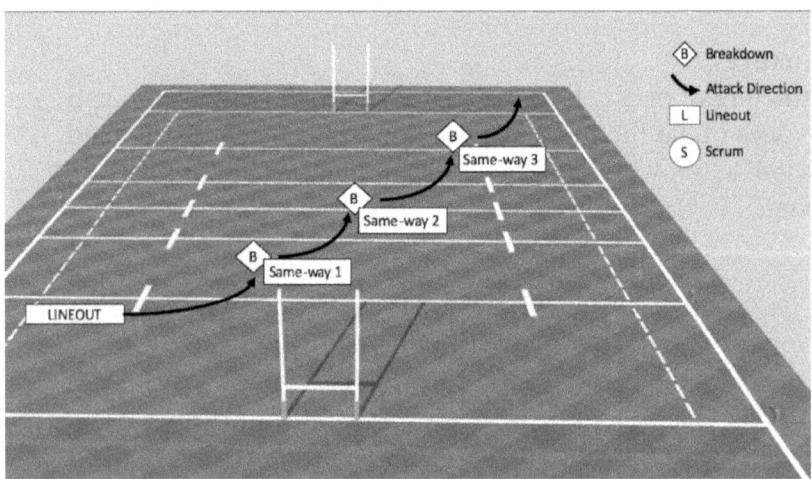

Develop A Player

An attacking structure that goes the same way twice and then rewinds once before repeating is commonly referred to as a '21' attacking pattern.

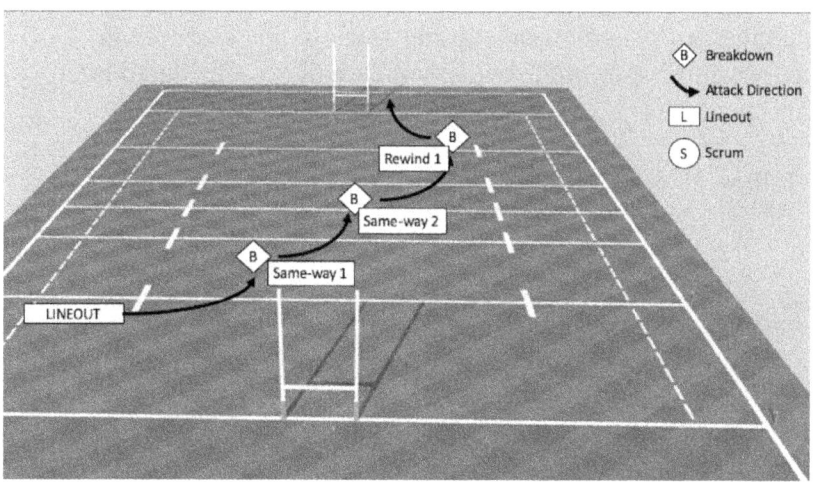

An attacking structure that goes the same way once and then rewinds once before reverting back to the same way is commonly referred to as a 'piston' attacking pattern.

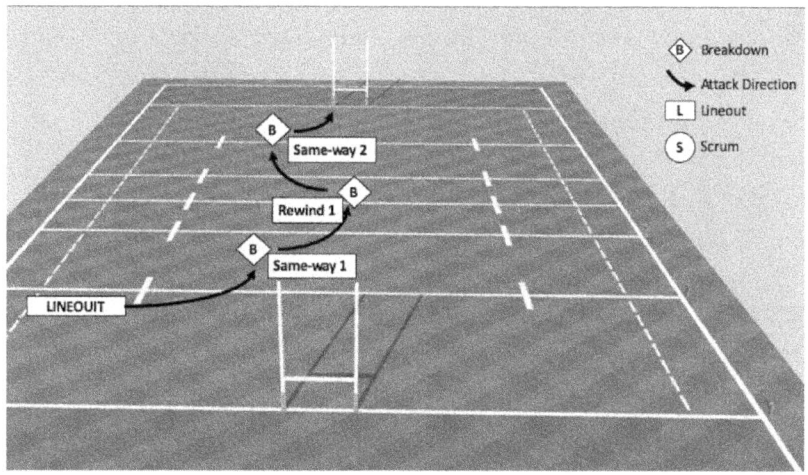

Develop A Player

Shapes

A shape is the pre-defined attacking position the players take up when executing a structured play. The following shapes are considered primarily from a forward perspective however in the modern game of rugby heads up rugby should be considered where scoring opportunities exist which will be considered later in this chapter.

The following is an example of a 1-3-3-1 attacking shape:

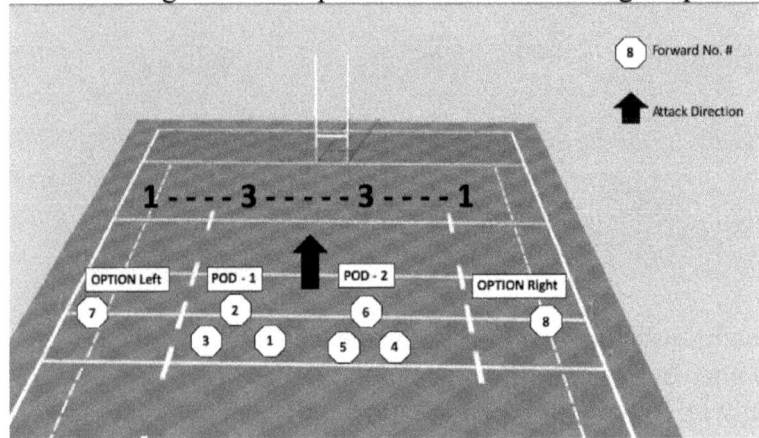

The following is an example of a 2-4-2 attacking shape:

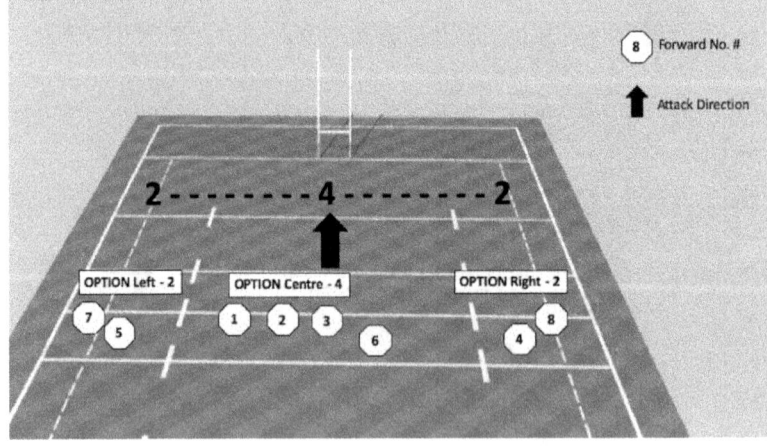

Develop A Player

Strategies and Tactics

Now, with an understanding of field segmentation, structures, and shapes, a coach can start to map a game plan to the competencies of the players.

To be successful in the execution of a game plan, the coach needs to not only consider which shape and structure to use but also the game conditions and the capabilities of the opposition.

When you start to add all these factors together, the coach can easily start to overthink the problem and become paralysed by the analysis. Therefore, the following basic success formulas can be considered as a solid foundation to develop further tactics.

Red zone Strategy plays

Objective: to move out of the zone, and play in either the blue zone or the green zone

Tactic: Use a 'Piston' structure with a 1-3-3-1 shape

Reason: The forwards can work in tight patterns around the breakdown being able to quickly reset

---

Blue zone Strategy plays

Objective: to move efficiently and effectively up the field and into the green zone for a scoring opportunity

Tactic: Use a '21' structure with either a 1-3-3-1 or a 2-4-2 shape

Reason: Attacking opportunities exist on both sides of the breakdown meaning that the opposition has to spread its defenders.

Develop A Player

> **Green zone Strategy plays**
>
> **Objective:** to secure scoring opportunity
>
> **Tactic:** Use an 'exhaust' structure with either a 2-4-2 shape
>
> **Reason:** The forwards can easily reset in the same attacking direction with an opportunity for a mismatch (attacking forwards against defending backs)

A multitude of shapes and structures can be developed with greater, and greater sophistication based on the capabilities of the players concerned in each game. Additional field segmentation can be added, and statistical analysis can be used to 'code' teams and individual players.

Learn to utilise and take advantage of every piece of information that is available but remember to take joy and happiness from becoming a deviant and master tactician in the wonderful game that is Rugby Union.

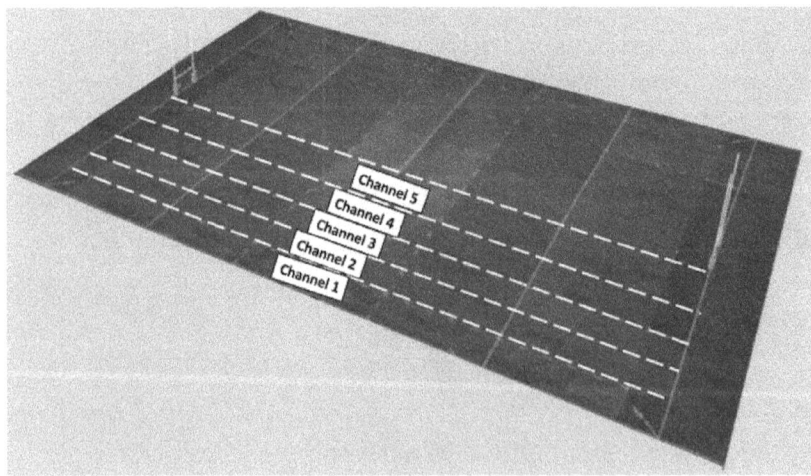

Develop A Player

How to maintain continuity of play

The term "open play" is known as the passage of play in the game when one team is attacking, and one team is defending.

This passage of play can be continuous until such point where there is an infringement that requires a restart through either a scrum, lineout, penalty or a score.

During the open play the objective of the attacking side is to achieve continuity with interchange between forwards and backs.

The front-row, and the second-row are the main contributors to the scrum and lineout restarts, which is why they are also referred to as the tight-forwards:

- *"Tight-forwards"* i.e. Loose-head Prop (LHP); Hooker (H); Tight-head Prop (THP); Loose-lock (LL); Tight-lock (TL).

The back-row are however the main contributors to open play rugby and are instrumental in maintaining the continuity of the attacking movement, which is why they are referred to as the loose-forwards:

- *"Loose-forwards"*: i.e. Blindside Flanker (BF); Openside Flanker (OF); Number Eight (8).

Now, Rugby Union is a game of evasion, skill, strategy and continuity, however contact situations occur all the time. Unlike Rugby League however the game continues after the contact situation has taken place, and therefore it is essential to understand the two ways in which contact can take place, but continuity of the attack can happen through either a "ruck" or a "maul".

Develop A Player

A ruck is formed if the ball is on the ground and one or more players from each team are on their feet close around it. Players must not handle the ball in the ruck and must use their feet to move the ball or drive over it so that it emerges at the team's hindmost foot, at which point it can be picked up.

A Maul takes place when the ball carrier is held, but not brought to the ground, a maul may be formed. For a maul to form there must be at least three players involved, including the ball carrier, an opponent holding the ball carrier, and a teammate of the ball carrier bound to the ball carrier. When a maul has formed, it must keep moving forward towards a goal-line. The players must stay on their feet. Once a maul has been formed, an offside line comes into force for both teams which is parallel to the goal-line and right behind the foot of the hindmost player in the maul.

Develop A Player

The purpose of both the "tight-forwards" and the "Loose-forward" is to know how to ruck and maul effectively in open play so that the continuity of the attack can be maintained.

By understanding open play rugby, and the continuity of attack a coach can then focus on tactics and strategies of teaching attacking rugby, and defensive rugby, and both those concepts will be discussed further throughout this book.

Pros' and Cons' of structure v heads up Rugby
Structure gives players a focus and a plan of action they can rely upon when defences do not offer easy opportunities to exploit.

Heads-up, free play allows athletes a chance to show their skill, both as individuals and combined in pairs, threes, or in larger collaborative units. Both attacking strategies have their limitations, however. Rigidly-structured play can make players to worry too much about their positioning within 'the plan', causing them to miss easy opportunities that emerge. Heads-up play can be random and hand initiative to the opposition, especially when individuals go alone, or players find themselves not knowing where to be. The obvious solution should be to combine the two strategies

This simple 'structure' is more of a guideline that gives players a clear idea of where to go and what they can do when they get there, but still allows them the freedom to exploit opportunities as they emerge and play to their strengths

This structure is based on an understanding that each set piece or breakdown has different attacking channels, each with its own possibilities and limitations. Heads up rugby sets the ground rules that if you believe a scoring opportunity exists from anywhere on the field then trust in your skill and rugby competencies to take advantage and achieve success.

Chapter 8:

Core skills

Chapter Objectives:
In this chapter you will gain knowledge of the following:

- ☑ **Catch and Pass skills development**
- ☑ **Tackling skills development**
- ☑ **Continuity skills development**
- ☑ **Kicking skills development**

Catch and Pass skills development
To become competent in the sport of rugby union, a developing player needs to learn how to catch and pass the ball at a proficient level, and to work within the team environment. To do this effectively the developing player needs to learn five types of basic passing.

- **Basic pass** - This is a very versatile pass that can be used in many situations. It allows you to easily control the speed and distance of the pass.
- **Long clearing pass** - This pass is used most often when you are the Scrum-half or the player acting in that role. You remove the ball from the base of the scrum or a ruck and send it out to the backs. If you position your feet and arms well in relation to the ball, you can pass swiftly, giving the receiver more time and space.
- **Close support pass** - You use two hands for this pass; gentle and soft to close players. Move your arms to disguise what you are doing, but supply power mainly

Develop A Player

with your fingers, giving great control over short distances.
- **Get out of trouble pass** - Useful when a long ground pass is required but you are not in the correct position to make one and are being pressured which prevents you from taking time to get set. A risky pass. Should only be attempted by the highly skilled in dire emergencies.
- **Over-head pass** - You use this pass to get the ball to a supporting player when there is an opposition player directly between you and your support. The lobbing motion allows the ball to travel in an arc above and out of reach of your opponent(s).

The mechanics of passing the rugby ball

To develop the skills of catch and pass there is nothing better than constant practice. The more you have the ball in your hands the more you will learn to be comfortable with the ball. Over time, muscle memory will be learned, and it will become a natural movement.

On the development journey to be able to easily and effectively catch and pass there are however three basic principles that, if followed, can develop these skills faster.

Firstly, you must have a great grip on the ball. The best players hold the ball with the fingers and thumbs. They can transfer the ball quickly from one to two to one hand. They can manipulate the ball around their body as they are running and stepping. That means they can pass in almost any direction.

Secondly, Use the body. A very short pass only needs the wrists, a longer pass might use elbows and twist of the shoulders, while a very long pass needs to engage the hips and use footwork.

Develop A Player

Finally, follow through. The hands finish towards the target or on the line of the target. The best way to check is to see where the middle finger is pointing at the end of the pass.

Now you have a template to work to, concentrate on what really matters. Starting with grip, work on catching the ball first but developing players need to work on adjusting the ball in their hands so that it feels natural. When it feels natural, then the player can make the best possible pass.

Tackling Skills Development
Tackling is one of the absolute fundamentals of rugby and as such needs to be learned, re-enforced and continuously worked upon during a player's career. If the technique is learned safely and thoroughly at an early age, then that player will always be able to execute the skill and take joy from that part of the game.

Front on tackle (passive)
This tackle is commonly referred to as the sacrifice tackle. If perfected, it will be achieved every time, regardless of the opponent's size, height, and strength.

To successfully execute this technique the following process is followed:
- Imagine the target on the bottom of the ball carrier's shorts.
- When tackling, keep the head up and with the chin of the chest.
- Brace the shoulders.

Develop A Player

- Make initial contact with shoulders on the ball carrier's thigh.
- Keep the arms around the carrier's legs.
- Keep the head up and to one side of the ball carrier's legs.
- Use momentum to take the ball carrier over the shoulder.
- Twist around and land on top of the tackled player.
- Get up immediately after the tackle and compete for the ball.

Front on tackle (active)
The objective of this tackle is to drive the ball carrier behind the advantage line. To successfully execute this technique the following process is followed:
- Get the lead foot as close as possible to the ball carrier.
- Keep eyes on the point of contact.
- Keep head to one side.
- Drop hips to lower the centre of gravity.
- Drive shoulder up to the centre of the target either into the stomach or onto the chest.
- Power comes from an explosive drive upwards emanating from the legs and buttocks.
- Wrap the arms around the player.
- If possible, pick one leg up.
- Keep driving until the attacking player's balance is broken and you are in control of his body.
- Continue forward landing onto of the attacking player.
- Get up immediately after the tackle and compete for the ball.

Side on tackle
This kind of tackle requires the tackler to anticipate the future point of contact and then track the ball carrier. Once the tackler

Develop A Player

has positioned the ball carrier into the desired position, then the following process should be followed:
- Get the lead foot as close as possible to the ball carrier.
- Imagine the target on the bottom of the ball carrier's shorts.
- When tackling, keep the head up and with the chin of the chest.
- Brace the shoulders.
- Make initial contact with shoulders on the ball carrier's thigh.
- Keep the arms around the carrier's legs.
- Keep the head up and to one side of the ball carrier's legs.
- Use momentum to take the ball carrier over the shoulder.
- Twist around and land on top of the tackled player.
- Get up immediately after the tackle and compete for the ball.

Rear tackle

This tackle requires the tackler to anticipate the future point of contact and possess an attitude that means he never gives up. A rear tackle is normally used when an attacker has broken the gain line and is heading for the try line. It's not so much about ability, it's about attitude and commitment. Once the tackler has got close enough to the ball carrier, then the following process should be followed:

- Get the lead foot as close as possible to the ball carrier.

Develop A Player

- Imagine the target on the bottom of the ball carrier's shorts.
- When tackling keep the head up and with the chin of the chest.
- Brace the shoulders.
- Make initial contact with shoulders on the ball carrier's thigh.
- Keep the arms around the carrier's legs.
- Keep the head up and to one side of the ball carrier's legs.
- Drive with the legs, gripping with arms and hands to bring the ball carrier to the ground.
- Land on top of the tackled player.
- Get up immediately after the tackle and compete for the ball.

Smother tackle
The idea of the smother tackle is to wrap the ball carrier up so that he can neither pass the ball nor release the ball. This kind of tackle should be taught to players who are already proficient in the other forms of tackling rather than use it as the primary tackle technique. To successfully execute this technique the following process is followed:
- Get the lead foot as close as possible to the ball carrier.
- Keep eyes on the point of contact.
- Wrap the arms around the upper part of the ball carrier's body.
- Trap the ball and the player's arms.
- Add your own weight to the ball carrier and bring the player to the ground.
- Land on top of the tackled player.

Continuity Skills Development

A breakdown happens when there is a stop in the forward momentum, but the ball is still live and in active play. As discussed in the previous chapter the key is to maintain continuity of the attacking movement and this can be done in three ways.

- **Tackle off-load** – As the attacking player is tackled his first consideration to maintain the continuity in play is to look for an offload. If the opportunity exists, then the off-load pass should be considered. If there is any doubt, then either of the following two options exist to maintain possession of the ball and keep the attacking movement going.

- **Ruck** - A ruck is formed if the ball is on the ground and one or more players from each team are on their feet close around it. Players must not handle the ball in the ruck and must use their feet to move the ball or drive over it so that it emerges at the team's hindmost foot, at which point it can be picked up.

- **Maul** – When the ball carrier is held, but not brought to the ground, a maul may be formed. For a maul to form there must be at least three players involved, including the ball carrier, an opponent holding the ball carrier, and a teammate of the ball carrier bound to the ball carrier. When a maul has formed, it must keep moving forward towards a goal-line. The players must stay on their feet. Once a maul has been formed, an offside line comes into force for both teams which is parallel to the goal-line and right behind the foot of the hindmost player in the maul.

Develop A Player

Kicking Skills Development
As the game of rugby develops, so does the need to be comfortable in all aspects of the game. There are only three reasons why kicking should take place on a rugby field; to restart play, to gain territory or to score a try.

In the modern game we see teams kicking from all areas of the field as they try to exploit the space left by defenders. Gone are the days of only kicking for territory. The modern kicker must, therefore, be able to master four basic types of kicks
- The distance kick
- The cross-field kick
- The grubber
- The chip
- The conversion

The distance kick
For a kicker, it is crucial that they can execute a competent end-over-end kick. This kick is often used to gain territory, especially when trying to relieve pressure from deep within their half. It is also a most effective kick when aiming to catch the opposition off guard with a cross-field kick. The basics of the kick are simple. The ball is caught and held with an excellent "W" position.

The non-kicking foot is grounded, the kicking leg strikes the ball on the point of the ball, and a high follow-through should follow.

Head stays down over the ball as arms lift and finishes in a position in line with where the ball has landed. A player should ensure they kick the ball with the laces of their boots (the middle of the foot).

The cross-field kick
The cross-field kick is a great attacking option for a kicker. This kick requires plenty of communication and pinpoint accuracy. The kick is often best performed while on the move. The catch is crucial, and to get the ball where they want it to go with the kick, the player must ensure their hips are in line with where they want the ball to end up. Alignment of the hips to where the ball should land is an essential part of properly executing the kick.

As the kicker, you want to be able to put enough flight and height on the ball to enable your outside backs to compete. The better cross-field kicks ensure the ball is in front of your players, so they are running onto it, this gives your team an advantage over defenders as they are on the front foot. They run with purpose and can perform a jump from a running start, not a static position which a defender may find themselves in.

The grubber kick
The grubber is a highly efficient kick for many reasons. It can be used when under pressure, and to turn the opposition's defence. It is also a great tactic to use when wishing to manage the time left in the game.

Often a team will drill the ball into touch to form a set piece and re-organise their defensive system. It is also used in attacking situations to score tries and fly hack the ball when it is loose on the ground.

Develop A Player

The key to executing an effective grubber is the angle of the ball when it is kicked.

The chip kick
The chip is a highly effective kick for a kicker to execute. Often a defensive back three will set up deep in defence, meaning a distance kick is hard to accomplish. The chip kick can be performed to get over the gain line. Often, if this kick is efficiently executed, a defensive team will bring their back three up in the hope it will prevent a kicker from continuing to implement it.

The chip is also a great way of attacking against a blitz defence or in a one-on-one situation. To perform this kick effectively, you will execute it on the move. The chip kick is a harder kick as you have to catch, kick, run and collect all in a matter of seconds.

The best way to perfect this kick is to practice against a pressured defence. The kick is again performed in the middle of the foot. Ensure the release of the ball is below knee height, which allows power to be pushed into the ball. Whether the kicker kicks from front on or sideways depends on the situation but having enough flight to regain or contest possession is crucial to this kick.

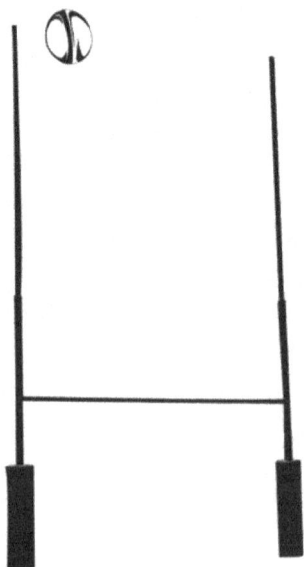

The conversion
At higher levels of play, coaches look at conversion success rate when recruiting players.

Develop A Player

In the modern day, you see an array of kicking styles and stances. Firstly, the non-kicking leg should be grounded next to the ball on the tee with your eyes and head firmly looking at the ball.

As you kick, ensure you do so with the middle of the foot for a strong follow through. A good practice drill is to stand on the try line facing the rugby sticks. Of course, you can only see the one on the side you are on.

From here practice kicking the ball off the tee, this will help work on your accuracy. The power will develop with technique, age, and specific training.

Other kicks

- **The drop kick** - Not only is this style of kick a way of restarting play, but it is also an opportunity to score points. The kicker is often tasked with restarting the game as they can dictate where they want the ball to go as well as organise a defensive line from there. So, kicking the ball into the right areas is crucial for strategic point scoring and tactical territory gains.

- **A restart from the halfway line** - Usually, you will try to aim as close as possible to the touchlines ensuring the ball travels 10 meters. This gives your team a chance to compete for the ball. Alternatively, you will kick deep and organise a strong kick chase. This ensures a team has to play from deep within their half or kick for territory.

- **A restart from the 22-meter line** - Usually, you will try to aim as close as possible to the touchlines,

Develop A Player

however, the ball only has to cross the 22-meter line. The kicker has the option to kick short in an attempt to regain the ball or kick deep and organise a strong kick chase.

Chapter 9:
Essential skills for developing players

Chapter Objectives:
In this chapter you will gain knowledge of the following:

- ☑ **Attacking Rugby**
- ☑ **Defensive Rugby**
- ☑ **Physical Conditioning**
- ☑ **Mental Strength**
- ☑ **The influencers on the four disciplines**

Background
In the modern era of rugby union, there is considerable emphasis put on size, strength, genetic make-up and aggression. This emphasis is detrimental to the young player.

It is true that at the highest level of professional rugby and international competition, size does matter. Gone are the days when front row players had a certain shape, second row players were the tallest on the field and wingers were speedsters with little or nothing in the way of bulk muscle.

That being said, there are exceptions to size. If we look deeper than just the physical appearance, we can see the journey these players have been on which led them to become the top players in their current positions.

Develop A Player

Rugby union is seen by many as a complicated game of massive collisions, infringements, stoppages and periods of no action. Others see the sport as a strategic movement of players in complex formations achieving superiority in numbers in certain regions of the pitch, which leads to scoring opportunities. Both perspectives can be true, but there are a multitude of additional interpretations in-between.

We need to help young players entering the game of rugby union understand that the game is actually one to be enjoyed. We need to help them understand it is a game of strategy, evasion and the core disciplines of attack and defence, but also of physical and mental conditioning. If the young athletes can understand these aspects, and execute them with pace, power, agility and skill, then irrespective of their size, or strength, they can compete at the highest level of Rugby Union and reap the emotional and social benefits of success.

Attacking rugby
Attacking rugby can be broken down into two scenarios; when you have the ball in your possession and when you don't.

Attacking with the ball in possession

When you have the ball in your possession you have the advantage. Sometimes young players forget that and start to panic, which leads to mistakes in running, passing and catching. If you are attacking with the ball, then the opposition needs to react and try to stop you. If you can attack quicker, with greater skill and more purpose, the outcome will be positive.

The ability to attack with confidence stems from three simple building blocks:
- Attack space (***knowledge***).
- Know you can execute a skill with confidence and precision (***practice***).
- Keep focused and be in the moment (***commitment***).

Attacking without the ball in possession

Due to the fluidity of the game, the conditioning, and the number of players on the field, the support role of team members in attack is equally as essential as the primary attacking player himself.

In younger age groups, if a player breaks through a tackle-line they tend to run the length of the playing area and score. However, as the size of the playing area, and the number of players on the field increases, the defence tends to regroup to stop the breakaway score. This means that attacking without the ball in possession is equally as important which is referred to as support play.

The ability to attack without the ball in position, therefore, comes down to three key aspects:
- Anticipating where the likely contact point with the defence will be and be in position to keep the attacking movement going (***support***).

Develop A Player

- Providing options for attacking continuity (***understanding***).
- Decide what the best role will be in providing those support options for attacking continuity (***be a team player***).

Defensive rugby
Defensive play has evolved dramatically in recent times, primarily down to the influence of other sports. Defensive structures, defensive roles, and defensive policies have all played a major part in the modern game of rugby union, leading to more strategic thought on how to break down those defensive patterns.

It is important to also understand where attacking sides are most likely to score, and then develop a defensive policy in response, but not at the expense of the natural skills and flair of players being able to defend instinctively.

To understand how and when to defend effectively statistical analysis is very important. If we look at the 2014 statistics information from the southern hemisphere Super 16 sides where tries were scored some interesting insights can be drawn.

Team	From own lineout	From own scrum	From restart receipts	From open play - tap	From kick receipts	From turnovers
Blues	23	13	12	4	28	19
Brumbies	25	6	15	1	34	19
Bulls	23	9	12	2	33	21
Cheetahs	22	5	12	5	34	22
Chiefs	18	12	13	4	29	24

Crusaders	20	10	14	2	36	18
Highlanders	18	11	13	3	33	22
Hurricanes	16	11	14	3	33	23
Lions	25	10	13	3	26	22
Rebels	21	13	13	4	31	19
Reds	24	12	10	3	29	23
Sharks	21	9	13	2	36	20
Stormers	22	11	10	2	33	20
Waratahs	19	13	15	4	27	23
W-Force	22	12	10	3	33	21
Average	**21**	**10**	**13**	**3**	**32**	**21**

From reviewing this kind of data, we can start to identify insights on what to defend and why thereby providing a competitive edge over the opposition. For example, if we were to use the above data to develop our defensive policy, we could conclude that if a team was to defend well from kick receipts, lineouts and turnovers, then they would have statistically reduced the attacking sides' probability of scoring by 74%. We can, therefore, look at defence principles associated with set pieces and broken play to become more effective in this part of the game.

Defending set pieces
Set pieces are defined as either lineouts or scrums. Based on the statistics identified above, we would break each down into the elements and put in place defensive practices that would focus on the following:

- **Lineout Defence** – Look to defend the following areas:
  o At the point of catch in the lineout
  o On the short side of the lineout (between the touch line and the 5M line)
  o On the immediate open side of the lineout (between the 15m line and the goal posts)

Develop A Player

- o   On the far open side (between the goal posts and the opposite touch line)
- **Scrum Defence** – Look to defend the following areas:
- o   Defend the scrum by not retreating
- o   Within 2m of the scrum (both sides)
- o   Within 15m of the scrum (both sides

By looking at these specific aspects of set piece play we are identifying defensive channels. By understanding these channels, defensive patterns can be developed and adapted to counter sides that are more likely to attack from set pieces.

Defending broken play
Broken play defence is defined as either defending from when the ball has been kicked to the attacking team, or when the attacking team has maintained possession after a contact situation. By using the playing statistics identified earlier we would again look at defensive policies around the following:

- **Restart Receipts** – Look to defend the following areas:
- o   Within 10m of the attacker receiving the ball (to prevent momentum)
- o   Behind the first defensive line (in case of a line break)
- o   Deep (in case of chips, grubbers and territory advantage)
- **Tap** – Look to defend the following areas:
- o   Within 10m of the attacker receiving the ball (to prevent momentum)
- o   Within 15m of the tap (to prevent early line breaks)
- **Kick Receipts** – Look to defend the following areas:
- o   Within 10m of the attacker receiving the ball (to prevent momentum)
- o   Behind the first defensive line (in case of a line break)
- o   Deep (in case of chips, grubbers and territory advantage)
- **Turnovers** – Look to defend the following areas:

Develop A Player

- o Within 1m of the turnover (to counter pick and go)
- o Within 3m of the turnover (to counter first receiver)
- o Within 5m of the turnover (to counter first receiver running onto the ball at pace)

Physical Conditioning

Young rugby union players should find enjoyment in the game and be able to compete, and therefore a certain level of base conditioning is a very important factor that allows them to do so.

When considering the dynamics and body movements of a rugby player, it is interesting to know that the average distance a forward runs with the ball in hand during a game is between 5 to 10 meters in any one carry and that a back normally runs on

average between 10 to 30 meters. That doesn't seem like a lot and, in fact, it isn't when compared to athletics where kids run hundreds, if not thousands of meters in a single athletic race.

Rugby union, however, is unique in that it requires forwards and backs to perform those relatively short distances when the ball is in hand at 100% output, reload, and then go again.

Additionally, the sport requires the player to be operating at 60-70% of their maximum in support and then be able to immediately reach that 100% output the moment they have the ball in hand.

By understanding these dynamics, we can put in place the necessary conditioning that will help rugby athletes have the physical stamina necessary to perform in these attack and defence scenarios.

General physical conditioning
To get an idea of the general physical conditioning levels needed to perform in a particular playing position at a particular age, the Develop A Player organization has mapped out a number of range parameters. These are free and accessible through the Develop A Player web portal by setting up a free professional player profile (www.developaplayer.com/player/registration).

Additional, and specific physical conditioning for different playing positions is outlined in each of the player specific books which provides a deeper understanding of the conditioning needed for great rugby.

Mental Strength
Sports play a huge role in our society, and as such mental conditioning needs to be taken seriously as it can play a huge role in helping athletes achieve success. Participation in childhood sports can be a rewarding experience and a good introduction can lead to a lifetime of enjoyment.

For parents, coaches and support networks, understanding who understand mental development in young players can increase the player's overall involvement and enjoyment of sports. As the adults guiding children in sports, it is important for them to remember that, while there are some fundamental building blocks for success, no two people are completely alike.

Understanding a child's development helps adults avoid unnecessary frustration and inappropriate expectations while simultaneously creating an environment of learning, increased participation, and fun.

Young children (ages 7-10 years) face two major challenges in sports:
- Learning how to get along with friends.
- Learning how to interact with authority figures other than their parents.

At this young age, learning to cooperate within a team and compromising for the interests of someone else are major accomplishments. Children at this young stage of a sport are just beginning to develop the ability to see the world from the perspective of others. Parents and coaches should make a clear distinction between what is acceptable behaviour and what is not. Since the child is learning, we need to provide them with the opportunity to grow through guided trial and error. It is important to remember that fun, exploration, and developing a love of sports are key elements at this age. If competition and winning become the main themes, these are most likely fostered by adults, which means they should temper their competitive nature in the interests of the child.

Pre-adolescents (ages 10-13 years) face the social challenges of developing best friends and gaining acceptance from peers. Social relationships are one of the developmental milestones that this age group is navigating. They want to be part of a group and often fear being embarrassed. Developing a same-sex best friend is a major task of this social stage. Pre-teens tend to be loyal to their friends and make many decisions based on maintaining their friendships. "Sports hopping" is an example of a decision based on maintaining a friendship. Sports hopping occurs when a pre-teen changes sports or quits participating in sports because of friendships.

During the pre-teen phase of development, practices should be structured that allow for social interactions. Coaches often view social interactions at practices as 'goof off' time. Contrary to many coaches' beliefs, a practice which contains structured social interaction as part of a regular routine helps develop team relationships.

Adolescents (ages 14-18 years) face the developmental challenge of defining who they are and how they fit into the world. Identity development is a complex process that involves applying the training and teaching we have given them, while the teen is trying on different identities. The teen is attempting to discover who they are and clarify their values through exploring different facets of their personality. This process occurs as parents and coaches wring their hands and watch as their own hair turns grey in exasperation!

Often, we see the teen's identity search in the clothes they wear, the music they listen to, and the changes they make in who their peers are. Being tolerant of the adolescent while they try out new ideas is an important behaviour for parents and coaches. Tolerance for new behaviours is guided by the rules that the behaviours do not place the teen in danger or interfere with team rules and goals. The second major transition during the teenage phase is recognizing that sports is truly important in life.

The teen makes the transition in identity from 'I play rugby' to 'I am a rugby player.' Participation in sports and being an athlete becomes a significant piece of their identity. Helping the teenage athlete enhance the technical mastery of their chosen sport while supporting their growth as an individual, is a challenge facing both parents and coaches.

Regardless of an athlete's age, there are several common themes that relate to participation in the sport that should be considered;

- To have fun
- For fitness
- Being with friends
- To compete

The social aspect of sports and having fun is appealing to the young athlete. Competition or winning is not the predominant motivator.
Recognizing the young athlete's need for encouragement, socialization, and fun is paramount. If the young athlete develops a love of sports, then with support and a healthy coaching environment, the drive for competition and mastery naturally develops.

No matter the age of your young athlete, there are several simple keys that help sports participation and competition evolve naturally:

- Be supportive.
- Avoid TMTS (Too Much Too Soon); children's natural drive for competition will evolve as they age.
- Structure time to include social interaction and fun.
- Help your teen incorporate athletics as part of their identity by being positive.

The influencers on the four disciplines
Sports should be fun for kids. Treat sport as a game, it is not a business for kids.

Develop A Player

With all the money in professional sports today, it is hard for parents to understand that it is just good fun to young athletes. The primary goal should be to have fun and enjoy the healthy competition.

Young athletes compete in sports for many reasons. They enjoy the competition, like the social aspect, engage with being part of a team, and enjoy the challenge of setting goals. Parents and coaches may have a different agenda than your young athlete, and as such they need to recognize that it is their sport, and not that of the parent or coach.

Emphasize a mental focus on the process of execution instead of results or trophies. We live in a society that focuses on results and winning but winning comes from working the process and enjoying the results. Teach your young athlete to focus on the process of the challenge of playing one shot, one tackle, or one run at a time instead of the number of wins or trophies.

Parents and coaches are role models for young athletes. As such, you should model composure and poise on the sidelines. When you are at a competition, your young athlete will mimic your behaviour as well as other role models. You become a role model in how you react to a close race or the questionable behaviour of a competitor or official. Stay calm, composed, and in control during games so your young athlete can mimic those positive behaviours.

What are some of the things' parents can do to help their kids enjoy and succeed at sports?

5 Rules for supportive parents and care givers

Develop A Player

1. Do what you can to make sure your child is having a positive experience with coaches and teammates. The wrong coach can turn a kid off to a sport. Similarly, conflicts with teammates and peer pressure can make sports quite unpleasant. Help your child work out these interpersonal issues. In some instances, you may need to intervene or intercede on his behalf.
2. Try to determine if your child seems better suited for team sports or for individual sports. Some kids love the camaraderie of team sports. Others enjoy competing on their own. And of course, some kids like both.
3. Be sure to model good sportsmanship, grace, gentleness, and integrity on and off the athletic field. If you behave inappropriately at training and matches, your children are likely to do the same.
4. Lots of kids have difficulty managing busy schedules, which include games, practices, travel, family activities and schoolwork. In many instances, the parents and their kids are spread quite thin and can easily become overwhelmed. Help your child find a balance and make sure they do not have too much on their plates at any one time.
5. Be aware of burn out. If your child has lost some of their enthusiasm, and their performance has declined, your youngster may be burnt out. Talk with them to see if they need a break, a new challenge, or a different approach to their sport.

Develop A Player

Coaches

Take the time to reflect on why it is you coach. This is beneficial not only for personal growth but also in creating an awareness of changes in our motivation.

- Motivation (why we do what we do) affects our behaviour (what it is we do).

Therefore, changes in our motivation can be reflected in our behaviours and also in our wellbeing.

Research suggests that coaching for intrinsic reasons such as love, joy and passion is associated with better outcomes. These outcomes include the health and wellbeing of the coach, improved coach-athlete relationships, athlete motivation, satisfaction, and performance.

Three psychological needs have been identified as important in fostering greater intrinsic motivation for an activity. To what degree do you feel these needs are satisfied by your coaching work?

- The need for autonomy (the desire to feel that your actions emanate from your own choice)
- The need for competence (the desire to be good at the activity)
- The need for relatedness (the desire to be connected to others)

Those who feel they coach because they want to, are good at it. Coaching allows them to continue relationships within their sport and with their athletes, display more intrinsic motivation for coaching, and coach with a more autonomy-supportive style.

Therefore, being aware of why you coach your sport is an important and reflective practice.

Your coaching motivation plays a crucial role in the facilitation of a healthy coaching environment, both physically and psychologically. Working in an environment that supports your needs will help you get the best out of yourself as well as your athletes.

Sports coaches assist athletes in developing to their full potential. They are responsible for training athletes in a sport by analyzing their performances, instructing in relevant skills, and by providing encouragement. But you are also responsible for the guidance of the athlete in life and in their chosen sport.

Consequently, the roles of the coach will be many and varied, and range from instructor, assessor, friend, mentor, facilitator, chauffeur, demonstrator, adviser, supporter, fact finder, motivator, counsellor, organizer, planner, and even the fountain of all knowledge.

Develop A Player

In relation to sports, the role of the coach is to create the right conditions for learning and to find ways of motivating the athletes. For athletes who are already highly motivated, the task is to maintain that motivation and generate excitement and enthusiasm.

The coach will need to be able to: assist athletes in preparing training programs, communicate effectively with athletes, assist athletes in developing new skills and use evaluation tests to monitor training progress and predict performance.

The role of the coach can be seen as a very difficult task requiring a very special person, and therefore, they need to be ready to perform in this role.

Chapter 10:
My greatest players

Chapter Objectives:
In this chapter you will gain knowledge of the following:

- ☑ **My journey as a Coach**
- ☑ **The Forwards**
- ☑ **The Backs**

My journey as a Coach
Rugby Union is a game that I have played in one form or another since the tender age of 4 when I had my first rugby ball presented to me in 1976. From the first moment I held this odd shaped object I have been hooked on the game, the way it is played and what it has given me in terms of friendships all over the world.

The whole purpose of the company I set up, Develop A Player, was to help every developing player in the sport get access to great couching and direct sponsorship so that they can play the game they love for free.

The second reason I set up the sports echo-system was to help give players, coaches and supportive family members a central point whereby they can engage and share in the joys of becoming become truly exceptional in something they love.

Having been immersed in the sport of Rugby now for over 40-years it has been my objective to study and model excellence so that I may on-teach those attributes to players. In this chapter I

Develop A Player

will outline, on a position by position basis, who I believe are the greatest players to have played in these positions and my reasons for their selection.

Whereas I am sure all the readers of this book will not agree with them all, it will have at least given you some food for thought.

Happy reading my friends……

The Forwards
My greatest Loose-head Prop - LHP

- My number one choice of LHP has to be **Os du Randt (RSA)** -Tipping the scales at almost 20 stone and standing at 6'3", this behemoth of a man is one of the few to have won two rugby World Cups. He took the brunt of the force in the scrum for 13 years for his country, and is their highest capped forward ever, with 80 caps. Nicknamed "Ox" for his brute strength, du Randt came back from three years of injury and is deserving of his place as the greatest loose head prop of all time.

- My next top 3 are; **Tony Woodcock (NZ)** - Woodcock was a rock in the All Black scrum for six years. As well as being one of the strongest scrummagers in the professional era, he is also very able when it comes to open play. Next is **Tom Smith (SCO)** - His 61 caps for Scotland have helped Smith to become one of the greatest loose head props of all time, as well as going on two British and Irish Lions tours, making six appearances. He scored six tries in his 61 Scotland caps and scored eight tries in his 152 games for premier club Northampton Saints. At 5'10" he isn't the tallest, but his

Develop A Player

brute strength and power make him a fearsome scrummager. And making it to the top level of great LHPs' is **Gething Jenkins (WAL)** ....

- Other outstanding gentlemen who deserve an honourable mention are; Jack Mcgrath (IRL); Mako Vanipola (ENG); Rob Evans (WAL); Charlie Faumuina (NZ); Adam Jones (WAL) Wales; Carl Hayman (NZ); Syd Miller (IRL); Fran Cotton (ENG); Hannes Marais (SA; Ian McLauchlan (SCO); Ken Gray (NZ); Graham Price (WAL) and Robert Paparemborde (FRA)

My greatest Hooker - H

- **Sean Fitzpatrick** is without doubt to top the list. Natural leader Fitzpatrick is widely regarded as one of the greatest players ever and is a true legend of the sport. He was the Captain of the mighty New Zealand rugby team and had an international career that spanned twelve years, making 92 appearances, which included a world record of 63 consecutive Test matches and 51 as Captain. A born leader, master tactician and the toughest hooker ever saw he probably should have won more than just the one World Cup in 1987. Did you know: He was awarded the New Zealand Order of Merit in 1997 and since retiring has remained a presence in the sport.

- The next top 3 are; Former Springbok Skipper **John Smit** is remembered most for leading his country memorably to the Rugby World Cup title in 2007. He made 111 Test appearances for the Springboks, which includes appearing in a record 46 consecutive Test matches between 2003 and 2007. Next comes Argentina hooker **Mario Ledesma** has formed part of dominant pack during some of the most successful years in the country's rugby history. He made his international debut against Uruguay in 1996 and has gone on to win 77 caps for his country, playing at Rugby World Cups in 1999, 2003 and 2007. His main qualities are his mobility around the field and dogged workrate, and he is also more than proficient at the set-piece. The third to make the top tier is **Phil Kearns**. He was part of the highly successful Australia team of the 1990s, having represented the Wallabies in both the triumphant 1991 and 1999 World Cup campaigns. The world-class hooker represented his country on 67 occasions, and also captained Australia ten times.

- Other outstanding gentlemen who deserve an honourable mention are; Keith Wood (IRE), Brian Moore (ENG), Dan Coles(NZ), Bismark Du Plesis(RSA), Steve Thompson(ENG), Rapahael Ibanez(FRA), Jamie George(ENG), Rory Best(IRE), Agustin Creevy(ARG), Ken Owens(WAL).

My greatest Tight-head Prop - THP

- My number on choice of Tight-head prop is **Jason Leonard (ENG)** - just couldn't have a team without him. Jason Leonard is the greatest prop England have ever produced, and probably the greatest of all time. While a polite yet fun-loving gentleman off the field, on the field he got the job done better than anyone. Until George Gregan passed his total in 2005, Jason Leonard was the most capped player in International rugby history with 114 caps. He remains the highest capped Englishman ever. Despite this he only ever scored one try in his England career. Part of four World Cups and three Lions Tours while winning five caps, Leonard has seen it all and has won the biggest prizes international rugby has to offer: Grand Slams and, of course, the World Cup.

- My next top three are; **Wilson Whineray (NZ)** - The longest serving captain in the history of the All Blacks (seven years), despite having only an eight-year international career, Whineray is also widely regarded to be amongst the best captains they have ever had. Of his 32 Test matches he captained 30, scoring two tries in the process. In 2007 he was inducted into the IRB Hall of Fame, while he was inducted into the International Rugby Hall of Fame back in 1999. next comes **Syd Millar (IRE)** - The former Ireland prop and former chairman of the International Rugby Board, Syd Millar is an inductee to the International Rugby Hall of Fame. He won 37 caps as prop, and was probably even more successful after he retired. Millar has been both coach and manager of the British and Irish Lions, as well as coach of Ireland at the 1987 World Cup. He was also a player for the Lions on the 1968 tour of South Africa. The next in the top tier would be **Carl Hayman** who was capped 45 times by New Zealand but would have had many more had he not opted to head overseas. Unusually tall for a tight-head prop, at 6ft 4in, the former Otago and Highlanders powerhouse became the 1000th All Black when he made his debut against Samoa in 2001. His career ended on a high last year with another Champions Cup prize with Toulon, where he also gained French Top 14 titles.

- Other outstanding gentlemen who deserve an honourable mention are; Adam Jones(WAL), Fran Cotton(ENG), Hannes Marais(RSA), Ken Gray(NZ), Graham Price(WAL), Robert Paparemborde(FRA), Martin

Develop A Player

Castrogiovanni(ITA), Tadhg Furlong(IRE), Owen Franks(NZ), Ramiro Herrera(ARG)

My Greatest Loose Lock - LL
- My number on choice of Loose-lock is Iconic England legend **Martin Johnson** is widely regarded as one of the greatest locks to have ever played the game. He famously led England to glory at the 2003 Rugby World Cup and also captained the British & Irish Lions in 1997 and 2001 – the first player to have ever led the elite tourists twice. In a glittering career, Johnson was also part of two Grand Slam-winning England sides in 1995 and again as the Skipper in 2003. *Did you know:* Johnson was awarded an OBE by The Queen in 1997 but later honoured with a CBE in the aftermath of England's Rugby World Cup triumph in 2003.

- My next top 3 are; Inspiring Ireland and British Lions Skipper **Paul O'Connell.** He was one of the most consistent players in Northern Hemisphere rugby in the last ten years. The veteran warrior has won three Six Nations titles in the emerald green of Ireland including a Grand Slam triumph in 2009 as well as winning the Triple Crown four times in 2004, 2006, 2007 and 2009.The legend hung up his boots following the 2015 World Cup due to injury. Following him, comes **Nathan Sharpe** for the Wallabies. He went on to not only Skipper the Wallabies but also become one of their most consistently excellent players since the millennium. Sharpe's outstanding work ethic across the field was also recognised as he won the Australian Rugby Union Players' Association's 'Medal of Excellence' on three occasions, joining George Gregan as a three-time winner of the honour. The last in this tier would be **Brodie**

Develop A Player

Retallick who pulled the All Blacks jersey at age 21 and has established himself with his mobility and aerial skills. In he was named World Rugby Player of the Year after a highly imposing campaign. His great athleticism and rugged defence made him one the stars of the All Blacks 2015 Rugby World Cup triumph.

- Other outstanding gentlemen who deserve an honourable mention are; Willie John McBride(IRE), Brad Thorn(NZ), Eben Etzebeth(RSA), Maro Itoje(FRA), Gordon Brown(SCO), Fabian Pelous(FRA), Frik du Preez(RSA), Garreth Llewellyn(WAL), Kane Douglas(AUS), George Kruis(ENG), **Bethan Miles** (WAL/ENG/AUS)

My Greatest Tight Lock - TL
- My number on choice of Tight-lock is **John Eales.** Perfect is a hard word to describe someone as but John Eales was not far off and that is why we have ranked him maybe surprisingly as no.1. He had pretty much every skill the modern-day rugby play requires and was a born match winner. A true Australian sporting legend, Eales won two World Cups and played 86 times for his country, 55 times as captain. Rarely for a forward, he was also a goal-kicker, with his most memorable strike being a sideline penalty goal in the final minutes of a 2000 test to win the Bledisloe Cup against New Zealand.

- My next top 3 are; South Africa's **Victor Matfield** defined the attributes required to be a modern-day second row: tall, powerful, mobile and with great hands. During his 122 Test caps with the Springboks, he formed a formidable second-row partnership with Bakkies Botha that played a crucial role in South Africa claiming the

Develop A Player

2007 World Cup in France. Besides almost always winning his own line-out ball, Matfield is known for his exceptional skill at disrupting opposition line-outs, which was a key asset to the Springboks during their triumph in 2007. Next is **Sir Colin Meads** One of the legends of a golden era of amateur rugby, powerful lock Colin Meads' international career with New Zealand spanned an amazing 14 years. During that time, he won 55 caps and played a major part in series wins over all the major Test nations, as well as the British Lions. Meads has been received a number of honours for his contribution to the game. He has been inducted into the International Hall of Fame and the New Zealand Sporting Hall of Fame and in 1999 was voted the Player of the Century at an NZRU awards dinner. The next in to top tier is **Sam Whitelock.** The vastly experienced 28 year-old has racked up 73 caps since making his Test debut against Ireland in 2010, and was a key figure in New Zealand's successful 2011 and 2015 campaigns. Excellent in the lineout and superb in the loose, the Crusaders second-row is the epitome of the modern lock. Blessed with superb ball skills, a legacy perhaps of his basketball background, and a tireless engine, Whitelock is a class act.

- Other outstanding gentlemen who deserve an honourable mention are; Alun Wyn Jones(WAL), Lood de Jagar(RSA), George Kruis(FRA), Malcolm O'Kelly(IRE), Bill Beaumont(ENG), Sir Brian Lochore(NZ), Bakkies Botha(RSA), Luke Romano(NZ)

Develop A Player

My Greatest Blindside Flanker – BF

- My number on choice of Blindside Flanker is **Richard Hill(ENG)** was known for his abrasive play with his hard hits and ball carries and dogged support play and work rate at the breakdown. Hill was a "silent assassin" for club and country for years. His incredibly consistent play ensured he was the only player never dropped during Sir Clive Woodward's tenure. He won 71 England caps, scoring 60 points, and was named on three British and Irish Lions Tours, winning five caps.

- My next top four are 3 are; **Jerome Kaino(NZ),** A big game player with 60 Test caps, Kaino was the man of the match on his All Blacks debut in an uncapped game against the Barbarians at Twickenham. Known for his versatility and speed, and at age 32, Kaino is an integral component to the current All Blacks. Next comes **Francois Pienaar (RSA)** For all of his 29 Test caps between 1993 and 1996, Francois Pienaar captained the Springboks – his biggest occasion being to victory in the 1995 World Cup final. It was a remarkable feat for the Springboks and their leader who went into their first World Cup seeded ninth but beat defending champions Australia. They went on to defeat the All Blacks at the final. Last to this tier is **Owen Finegan(AUS)**, nicknamed 'Melon', debuted for Australia against Wales in 1986. He earned 56 Test caps in a career that culminated with him scoring a try in injury time of the 1999 World Cup that Australia won. While he was the Australian player of the year in 2011, he missed out on selection for the 2003 World Cup in Australia.

- Other outstanding gentlemen who deserve an honourable mention are; Jerry Collins(NZ), George Smith(AUS),

Jean-Pierre Reaves(FRA), Michael Jones(NZ), Simon Poidevin(AUS), Finlay Calder(SCO), Michael Hooper(AUS), Juan Martin Fernandez Lobbe(ARG), Francois Louw(RSA), Steffon Armitage(ENG).

My Greatest Openside Flanker – OF

- My number on choice of Openside Flanker is undoubtedly **Richard McCaw(NZ)**, or 'Richie' as he is widely known, is captain of the All Blacks and is generally recognised as the world's best openside flanker. His record as a player and as a captain is without precedent. He became the first All Black to reach 100 Tests in 2011 and by the end of the 2014 season, he had played 137 Tests (coming off the bench just six times), and was Captain in 100 Tests. McCaw reminded the world of his brilliance as a leader when he lifted the Webb Ellis Cup in 2011

- My next top four are 3 are; **Wavell Wakefield (ENG)** - Probably the most important figure in the development of back row forwards, Wakefield used his athletic skills to change the flanker from a static player to one who constantly pressurised the opposition half-backs and supported attacks in open play, as well as the standard winning of the ball in rucks. Next in line **Jean Prat (FRA)** - A 2001 inductee into the International Rugby Hall of Fame, Prat was a fantastic all-round player. He scored 139 points in his 51 French caps, in ways ranging from wonderful tries to conversions. Prat also captained his French side from 1954 onwards, and is an inductee into the International Rugby Hall of Fame. The last into this tier is **Sam Warburton(WAL)** who is one of the new stars of the international game having emerged as a world-class talent with a string of eye-catching displays

Develop A Player

for Wales. He captained Wales at the 2011 World Cup, the youngest player to do so, and was a key figure in their outstanding run to the semi-finals.

- Other outstanding gentlemen who deserve an honourable mention are; Dave Gallaher(NZ), Fergus Slattery (IRE), Ian Kirkpatrick (NZ), Ruben Kruger(RSA), David Pocock(AUS), Neil Back(ENG), Schalk Burger(RSA), Sam Cane(NZ), Chris Robshaw(ENG), Sean o'Breine(IRE).

My Greatest Number 8 – 8

- My number on choice of Number 8 is **Zinzan Brooke**. A brilliant all-round player who spent a decade at the top with the All Blacks. He made 58 test appearances, scoring 89 points. He scored 17 tries in test matches throughout his career, which was then a world record for a forward. He was a part of three World Cup squads, including the victorious 1987 group. In the 1995 World Cup he famously kicked a 50-metre drop goal—something most fly-halves have trouble doing—showcasing his wonderful all-round skills and supreme confidence. It is this confidence in his ability and his fantastic all-round ability that makes him the greatest No. 8 of all time.

- My next top four are 3 are; **Lawrence Dallagio**(ENG), One of the most decorated players in history, he has done it all in his career. He has won five Premiership crowns, three Powergen Cup trophies, two Heineken Cup medals, and a Parker Pen Challenge Cup with Wasps. With England he won four Six Nations and of course the 2003 World Cup. He won 85 England caps, scoring 85 points, and has been on three British and Irish Lions Tours. Next

Develop A Player

comes **Wayne Shelford (NZ)** - Another former captain of his country, the All Blacks didn't lose a single game while Shelford was at the helm. He is credited with bringing about the improved Haka to strike more fear into their opponents before they even started the game. In 1987, Shelford was a key member of the All Blacks team which triumphed in the first ever Rugby World Cup. The last in this top, The late Wales and British Lions **Mervyn Davies** is the only player on this list from the pre-World Cup era. Fondly remembered as Wales' greatest skipper, Davies was forced to retire from the game at the age of 29 after suffering a brain hemorrhage playing for Swansea. He was never dropped by Wales and was an OBE and member of the IRB Hall of Fame.

- Other outstanding gentlemen who deserve an honourable mention are; Sergio Parisse(ITA), Dean Richards(ENG), Hennie Muller(RSA), Morne du Plessis(RSA), Scott Quinell(WAL), Imanol Harinordoquy(FRA), Kieran Read(NZ), Jamie Heaslip(IRE), David Pocock(AUS), Billy Vunipola(ENG).

The Backs
My Greatest Scrum-half – SH

- My number on choice of Scrum Half is **Gareth Edwards(WAL).** He was notorious for his pace but also had an unexpected strength for a leaner player. He made 53 caps for Wales as well as making ten appearances for the British & Irish Lions, featuring on tours in 1968, 1971 and 1974.

- My next top four are 3 are; **Joost van der Westhuizen(RSA).** The scrum-half had all the skills but combined them with an almost pathological refusal to be

Develop A Player

dominated on the rugby field. The intelligent tactician played a key role in the Springboks' 1995 World Cup triumph in South Africa. He scored a fantastic 38 tries in 89 Tests. Next is **George Grega(AUS)**. He represented Australia 139 times and captained the side in a record 59 matches. The diminutive scrum-half took part in four World Cup campaigns including the 1999 triumph as well as the side that came heartbreakingly close in 2003. The last to the tier is **Nick Farr-Jones(AUS).** Equipped with an accurate, bullet-like pass and outstanding tackling skills, he made his Test debut in November 1984 against England at Twickenham. This appearance would be the first of 63 Tests he played between 1984 and 1993, which included him Skippering the Aussies to glory at the 1991 World Cup when they overcame England in the final.

- Other outstanding gentlemen who deserve an honourable mention are; Matt Dawson(ENG), Will Genia(AUS), Augustin Pichot(ARG), Justin Marshall(NZ), Terry Holmes(WAL), Fourie du Preez(RSA), Greig Laidlaw (SCO), Niko Matawulu (FIJI), Ben Youngs (ENG), Aaron Smith (NZ)

My Greatest Outside-half – OH
- My number on choice of Outside Half is **Dan Carter(NZ).** The kiwi has established himself as one of the greatest players in history, being near faultless in every department: he can attack, break the line and kick accurately tactically or at goal. The incomparable All Blacks playmaker, former vice Captain and top points' scorer set a new international point-scoring record during New Zealand's triumph at the Rugby World Cup 2011. He has also won an incredible eight Tri-Nations/The

Develop A Player

Rugby Championship's as well as a series victory over the British and Irish Lions in 2005.

- My next top four are 3 are; **Jonny Wilkinson(ENG).** Forever remembered as the man whose last-gasp drop-goal won England the Rugby World Cup by edging past the hosts in Australia in 2003. That moment is just one highlight of a record-breaking career that has seen Wilkinson rise to one of the sport's all-time greats. England won 67 of the 91 games Wilkinson played in with him scoring an outstanding total of 1,179 points. He also holds the Rugby World Cup points record with 277. Next comes **Jonathan Davies(WAL).** Cross-code star Jonathon Davies made up for his lack of height, standing 5ft 8in, with great pace, great acceleration and natural quality. During his two periods in Union, he made a total 37 appearances for Wales and is considered one of Wales's finest ever rugby talents. The last to the tier is **Michael Lynagh(AUS).** For a decade from his debut in 1984 to his international retirement in 1995, former Wallaby Skipper Michael Lynagh was one of the most distinguishable players in World Rugby. After 72 internationals, he had set a new point-scoring record of 911, which is still an Australia record.

- Other outstanding gentlemen who deserve an honourable mention are; Naas Botha(RSA), Hugo Porta(ARG), Grant Fox(NZ), Jonathan Sexton(IRE), Mark Ella(AUS), Barry John(WAL), Neil Jenkins (WAL), Phil Bennett (WAL), Andrew Mehrtens (NZ), Ollie Campbell(IRE), Cliff Morgan(WAL).

Develop A Player

My Greatest Inside Centre – IC

- My number on choice of Inside Centre is **Tim Horan(AUS).** Only a handful of players have won the Rugby World Cup twice (1991 and 1999) and the 80 times-capped Australia centre Tim Horan is among this exclusive club. Horan shot to prominence at the end of the 1980s and made his name in a centre pairing with Jason Little (also a two-time Rugby World Cup winner), a partnership that had started in schoolboy rugby and would go on to represent Australia with distinction for over a decade.

- My next top four are 3 are; At the Top is **Jeremy Guscott (ENG).** Guscott burst onto the International Rugby scene, scoring a hat-trick on his debut. This was a sign of things to come as he won 65 caps for England, scoring 143 points. His fluent and evasive running coupled with his hard tackling secured him a place on three Lions tours, where he won eight caps. Next comes **Mike Gibson (IRE)** - A highly versatile player, Gibson played for his country in four different positions, but it was at centre where he was his most devastating. His 15 year international career won him 69 Ireland caps, a record which stood until 2005 when Malcolm O'Kelly surpassed it. The last to the tier is a present All Black One of the stars of the modern game, **Sonny Bill Williams,** has achieved numerous amazing things in his sporting career. He has been a dual international and a national and international champion across different sports including rugby, league and boxing.

- Other outstanding gentlemen who deserve an honourable mention are; Will Carling(ENG), Damian de Allende(RSA), Jonathan Joseph(ENG), Ma'a Nonu(NZ),

Matt Giteau(AUS), Jamie Roberts (WAL), Jean de Villiers(RSA), Tevita Kuridrani(AUS), Danie Gerber(RSA), Wesley Fofana(FRA), **Alex Miles (ENG/WAL/AUS)**

My Greatest Outside Centre – OC

- My number one choice of Outside Centre is **Philippe Sella (FRA)** - He was as majestic as they game on a rugby pitch. Sella could make something out of nothing whenever he got the ball, be it with his blistering pace, his deceptive strength, or his fantastic rugby brain. He won 111 caps for France, a world record at the time, and scored 125 points in his 13 year International career. Sella is one of few players to have scored a try in every game of a Five Nations series. In 1999 Philippe Sella was inducted into the Hall of Fame, and he has secured his status as the best centre of all time.

- My next top four are 3 are; **Bruce Robertson(NZ),** They call him the Prince of Centres. One of the greatest All Blacks of all time, Robertson had the most complete game of any player on this list. With ball in hand he was threatening, possessing plenty of pace and the intelligence to know when and how to use it. He was exceptionally good at beating his man on the outside and had a great pass that could set up his wingers outside him. Next comes **Tana Umaga(NZ).** His impact on his team was huge and he was rarely bettered by an opponent. That's the career of Umaga in a nutshell. He was a complete player, capable of dangerous attack and brutal defence, while also possessing a cool head that saw him a good decision-maker and inspirational leader. The last to this tier is **Brian O'Driscoll(IRE).** There is a pretty good argument that Brian O'Driscoll is the best

Develop A Player

European rugby player this century. He and Jonny Wilkinson would fight for that honour, and O'Driscoll would certainly have his fair share of backers. Indeed there are many who would claim that the great man should be at the very top of this list.

- Other outstanding gentlemen who deserve an honourable mention are; Jason Little(AUS), Danie Gerber(RSA), John Dawes(WAL), Conrad Smith(NZ), Frank Bunce(NZ), John Gainsford(RSA), Brian Lima(SAMOA), Stirling Mortlock(AUS), Will Carling(ENG), Scott Gibbs(WAL).

My Greatest Blindside Winger – BW

- My number on choice of Blindside Winger is **David Campese(AUS).** In his 101 Australia caps he amassed 64 tries, which was at the time an international rugby record, but is now second in the all-time list. Love him or hate him, Campese was such a danger to all defences he faced. He was the equal top try scorer in Australia's victorious 1991 World Cup campaign. His "miracle pass" to set up a try for Tim Horan against the All Blacks that year- which Australia went on to win - epitomised his considerable powers of invention and execution. He was subsequently named man of the tournament.

- My next top four are 3 are; **Jeff Wilson (NZ)** - The super-athlete, Jeff Wilson had it all. He was strong, fast, agile and a deadly finisher. He is sixth in the all-time list of try-scorers (44), and third in the All Blacks list. His 44 tries came in 60 test appearances, and he scored 234 points for New Zealand. Next comes **Daisuke Ohata (JAP)**. A Japanese in this countdown! Perhaps not as well known as he should be, Ohata is the leading try scorer in international rugby history. He has also done this in phenomenal style, scoring his world record 69 tries in a miraculous 58 tests. Had these figures been against higher class opposition, Ohata would probably make it to No. 1 on this list. Last to this tier is **Jason Robinson (ENG)** - He was known as "Billy Whizz" for his incredible pace and for his trademark sidestep. One on one, Robinson is as good as anyone. He is one of few players to have excelled in both Rugby Union and Rugby League. In his 56 test matches in an England shirt, he scored 30 tries, including the only try in the 2003 World Cup final, which England would go on to win.

- Other outstanding gentlemen who deserve an honourable mention are; Gerald Davies (WAL), Bryan Habana(RSA), John Kirwin(NZ), Julian Savea(NZ), Rupeni Caucaunibuca(SCO), Anthony Horgan(IRE), Manu Tuilagi(ENG), Tommy Bowe(IRE), Rieko Ioane(NZ), Liam Williams(WAL).

My Greatest Openside Winger – OW
- My number on choice of Openside Winger is **Jonah Lomu (NZ).** Lomu was a phenomenon. Never before and never since has someone had such a big impact on the game of rugby. He burst onto the scene as a truly spectacular physical specimen. A man as tall as most second-rows, as heavy as most props and faster than most wingers. A 20 stone man who could run the 100 metres in 10.89 seconds. We had never seen anything like it. If he couldn't run past you, which he normally always could, he would just go through you, failing that, his hand-off was one of the finest ever seen in rugby history.

Develop A Player

- My next top four are 3 are; **Rory Underwood (ENG)** - England's record ever try scorer with 49 tries, if you count his one try for the Lions then Underwood is the third highest try scoring player in international rugby history. His 85 international caps (then an England record) included three World Cups, including helping England to the 1991 World Cup final. Next comes **Doug Howlett (NZ).** To be New Zealand's highest ever try scorer considering some of the players they have had, you have to be really good. And Doug Howlett is good. His 49 tries for the All Blacks in just 62 tests remains a record. The next to this tier **Shane Williams (WAL)** appeared 87 times for Wales from 2000 to 2011, scoring 58 tries Williams also made four appearances for the British and Irish Lions, three as a wing and one as a centre. Williams holds several other try records, both for Wales and internationally. His 30 tries away from his home country (including those at neutral sites) were the most for any playcr in history at the time of his retirement

- Other outstanding gentlemen who deserve an honourable mention are; Joe Rokocoko(NZ), Ieuan Evans(WAL), Nemani Nadolo (Fiji), Cory Jane (New Zealand), Leigh Halfpenny (Wales), Willie Le Roux(RSA), Christian Cullen(NZ), Tonderai Chavhanga(RSA), George North(WAL), **Max Miles (ENG/WAL/AUS)**

My Greatest Fullback – F

- My number on choice of Fullback is **Serge Blanco(FRA).** There could be only one-man top of this list, and that is Les Bleus legend Serge Blanco. The French icon's international career with France saw the flamboyant fullback perform various outlandish levels of

155

Develop A Player

skill while winning Five Nation Grand Slams in 1981 and 1987 as well as four further titles. Blanco was a threat from everywhere on the field and often took risks that we very rarely see nowadays. In total, he won 93 caps for France during his 11-year international career between 1980 and 1991, which was a record when he retired. He also scored an imposing 233 points and is a true legend of the sport.

- My next top four are 3 are; at the top **Percy Montgomery(RSA).** Bound to Springbok folklore, Percy Montgomery was the primary reason South African Rugby had so much success around the turn of the century, and it's earned him the number two spot on our list. Montgomery became the first Springbok to earn 100 caps and to this day remains their all-time top point scorer with 893 points in internationals. Next comes **Christian Cullen(NZ).** A record of 46 tries in 58 tests for the New Zealand national team remains one of the top 10 tallies for a player at the international level. It is also one of the most prolific ratios ever seen. The last to this tier is **Gavin Hastings(SCO).** A leader on and off the pitch Gavin Hastings was a jack-of-all-trades, specialising in both attack and defence. The former Scotland Skipper led his country in 20 of his 61 caps, which included the narrow Rugby World Cup semi-final defeat against England in 1991.

- Other outstanding gentlemen who deserve an honourable mention are; J.P.R Williams(WAL), Don Clarke(NZ), Andy Irvine(SCO), Leigh Halfpenny(WAL), Israel Dagg(NZ), Tom Kiernan (IRE), Gareth Thomas (WAL), George Nepia (NZ), Scott Spedding(RSA), Ben Smith(NZ), Israel Folau(AUS).

Other Books in the Series

The Front Row

  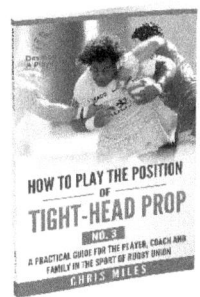

The Second Row

The Back Row

The Half-backs

The Inside Backs

The Outside Backs

About the Author

Chris Miles was born in Wales, UK in 1972 and started playing rugby at the tender age of 4. For the next 20-years he developed into an accomplished player gaining international rugby caps at junior and representative level for his country. A series of career ending injuries led him into coaching where he found his passion over the next 20-years developing rugby players. The author of 15-books covering every position on the field as well as the founder and architect of the Develop A Player rugby development ecosystem, and an ambassador for healthy and active kids in the field of sports.

The Development Portal

www.developaplayer.com

Develop A Player

www.ingramcontent.com/pod-product-compliance
Lightning Source LLC
Chambersburg PA
CBHW051839090426
42736CB00011B/1886